Contents

To a Dear Friend
who Loves

The Venice Project

Philip Gwynne Jones

Venice as I

c/o.

2014.

Brenda.

To my beloved wife Caroline, without whose love, support and courage The Venice Project, and this book, would have remained nothing more than a dream.

Introduction

At the end of 2011, my wife Caroline and I gave up our jobs in order to move to Venice.

We had no idea if it would be possible to live there full time, if we would be able to earn a living, whether homesickness would drive us back to the UK, or, indeed, how to go about a project like this.

I set to work trying to find some information that could help us, either in print or on the internet. I found numerous accounts of moving to Italy, but surprisingly few on Venice itself; and even fewer of those were from the perspective of 'normal' people - namely, those who would have to get a regular, non-glamorous job to make ends meet.

I decided that, whether it were to be successful or not, the whole experience would be worth recording, either as a 'how to do it' guide or as a terrible warning to others. In the event, the scope of the book changed as I wrote it, becoming, if you like, a diary of The Project and of our first year here.

It is not a history of Venice – the story of the Most Serene Republic has been written many times, and by writers far more adept than I. Neither is it an art, music or architecture primer. It is simply a record of what happened to us during the most extraordinary eighteen months of our lives; when everything changed on the basis of a conversation I once had with a man in a pub, and we went from being IT workers at a bank in Edinburgh to English teachers in the most beautiful city on earth.

This is the story of how we did it; and how we are still, just about, getting away with it.

Part 1

The Project

You can never know your own future...

Following years of carefree, feckless IT contracting, Caroline and I had decided that time was running out on us. We were middle-aged, we had nothing in the way of savings, we owned no property. We needed to start thinking about the future. We would buy a flat and get steady, secure jobs that would see us through to retirement and a comfy pension. A respectable, well-established, rock-solid business that we would be proud to say we were part of. We were going to do the right thing. The sensible thing.

We ended up working for the Bank of Scotland.

The roof fell in in 2008. Despite all assurances to the contrary, everyone at work knew that something was wrong. Every week, an email would arrive from the unlovely figure of chief executive Andy Hornby, assuring us that we were all doing very well and the bank was going from strength to strength. The big giveaway, however, was the attached photograph of Smiley Andy (imagine the rictus grin of Tony Blair channelling The Joker) suddenly changing to unsmiling, Serious Andy.

Then, one September afternoon, the BBC website reported that Lloyds were in discussion with the government with regard to a takeover. The site was quickly blocked and half-hearted denials were posted on the office intranet, but everybody knew what had happened: in the space of ten years, a bank that predated the Act of Union between England and Scotland had been run into the ground.

In late 2010 we were told that Caroline's job was at immediate risk and that mine would also be within twelve months. We faced redundancy, in middle-age, in a sector that was dying on its arse. Our flat was worth less than we had paid for it and our pensions were practically worthless. We had to face the fact that we had been rubbish at capitalism.

Except that, the more we thought about it, the more we

wondered quite why we would want to stay with the bank at all. Truth be told, it hadn't been much of a job for years and, following the takeover, things had become steadily worse. We saw a steady stream of friends and colleagues losing their jobs and any sense of job satisfaction was long gone, replaced only by the fear of redundancy. We worked in an industry that the public despised and for an organisation that gave every impression of being run by the greedy and the stupid. It had become, in short, a genuinely horrible place to work.

Why on earth, then, would we want to stay there? What if we were to try something else instead? Neither of us liked working in IT any more. So what if – with our redundancy money pooled – we tried something *really* different?

And this is where The Man in the Pub comes in.

A few years previously, I found myself in a pub in Glasgow meeting up with a group of people I'd come to know through a classical music forum. We talked about concerts, recordings and whether it was right for a pub in that particular part of the city to be offering such a thing as a 'Pint and Panini' (sic). Then it turned out that the meet-up was also a farewell party for one of our number.

He was leaving to move to Spain with his wife. He wasn't much older than me so I assumed he wasn't retiring. Indeed, it turned out they were going to teach English. Something called TEFL, which I soon found out stood for Teaching English as a Foreign Language.

I'd never heard of this before and thought little more of it until the following year when I ran into him once again, this time in a pub in Edinburgh. He was back to visit family for a couple of days. He talked about life in Spain. I moaned about work at the bank. He put up with this with remarkable patience, then went to the bar, returned with a pair of pints and smiled.

'Look Phil, you've got no kids. You've got no real ties here. You could do this as well, you know. What's keeping you?'

I never saw him again.

What if we were to try this in Italy? We'd always liked the idea of moving there, but it had never been more than the vaguest of dreams. In combination with this TEFL thing and a bit of redundancy money, might it be possible?

I spent hours upon hours running the figures through spreadsheets. We would clear our debts, use the remainder to move and then attempt to live off whatever teaching would bring in. The most basic of research indicated that this was not going to be a lot, but, with two of us working, it started to look feasible. We would have between one and two years of contingency to try to make it work.

There is no easy way to tell your wife that you've just had a life-changing idea based on a conversation with a man who you met in a pub two years previously. I was prepared to laugh it off as a silly joke on my part. And yet, when I explained the figures, Caroline just looked at me and said, '...so...we could actually do this?'

There was a lot to think about. We had a good life in Edinburgh. We had pubs, the theatre, concerts, galleries, plenty of friends. I liked the way we would run into people we knew simply by wandering about the town. I had lived there for nearly twenty years, longer than I had spent anywhere else in my life and the city fitted me like a comfy old pair of shoes. I had never imagined wanting to live elsewhere.

It was a lot to give up. Were we really going to do this, were we really going to take such a life-changing decision on the basis of something so uncertain? Yet there was something spine-tinglingly exciting about the whole idea.

There was no great moment of decision for us, but sometime in early 2011 we tacitly crossed the line from 'wouldn't it be great if we did this?' to 'we're actually going to do this!'

And so, The Project was born. The next time the bank held a round of voluntary redundancies, we would stick our hands up. We would pool whatever money they gave us and move to Italy to teach English.

It was not risk-free of course, but the risk-free path had led us to the financial services industry. If it worked, the prize was a great one. If it didn't, and we ended up back in the UK – well, we would at least have tried. There would never be a better opportunity of doing something like this.

There was also, of course, the risk of ending up broke and unemployable. We preferred not to think about that.

Why Venice?

We didn't come to Venice for Vivaldi, Gabrieli or Monteverdi. We didn't come for Titian, Tintoretto or Tiepolo. We didn't even come to have a gondola ride. We came for Gilbert and George.

Because our first visit to Venice, in 2005, was for the Biennale of Art. We had a week, and figured that would be enough. As it turned out, that was scarcely enough time to scratch the surface of the Biennale, let alone the city itself.

The strange thing is, Venice itself didn't make much of an impact on us. I came away with an impression of it being 'quite nice' but little more beyond memories of the suffocating heat of the Arsenale and aching feet. Still, we decided we should come back in a non-Biennale year and see what it was properly like.

Forward to 2006. Our flight from Naples had been delayed for hours. It was well past midnight when we arrived at Marco Polo airport. There were no boats running from there by that time and we didn't have the budget for a water taxi. So we took the bus to Piazzale Roma and then caught the night *vaporetto* to the Zattere, and our hotel.

It was 2:00am by the time we arrived and, fortunately, the

night porter was there to let us in. We scarcely had the energy to open a bottle of prosecco from the minibar before crashing out.

The next morning, I opened the curtains and there it was: the view across the Giudecca canal to Palladio's Church of the *Redentore*. The sun was shining on the water and I thought I had never seen a more beautiful city in my life. This was Venice, and I was finally beginning to understand it. We returned year on year, for longer and longer. If our Italian never improved very much, we started to feel at home in the city and to know our way around; and we could kid ourselves that having a bus pass was almost as good as being a resident.

At the end of our last holiday, in July 2011, we took the Alilaguna boat from the Zattere to Marco Polo. Caroline, somehow, snoozed the whole way. I leant my face against the window, watching as the city slipped from sight. The unbearable thought had occurred to me that we might never be able to return. If only one of us was able to lose their job, we wouldn't have enough money to fund the Project, and neither would we have enough to come back on holiday.

We had originally thought that we would go anywhere in Italy where we were able to find work, but no. It had to be Venice. It had to be the Venice Project.

Being Lucky

I'd been spreadsheet-pounding for weeks, trying to work out worst-possible-case scenarios along the lines of 'if we can't find work, how long before we have to give up?'

I looked at our redundancy pot and added in what we'd managed to save on overpaying the mortgage. Then I deducted the cost of clearing all our debts. Then I made a stab at estimating the likely living cost in Venice. Then I assumed that neither of us would be able to find work for a year.

It didn't leave a whole lot left over.

We could soften the blow by renting the flat out, but that still wouldn't be enough to cover the mortgage. Did we really want to be over a thousand miles away in the event of any problems with the flat or with the tenants? Would the fact that the rendering on the building needed to be replaced - a job that would involve months of scaffolding blocking out the view, hence ruining the flat's one real selling point - make it impossible to let anyway? There was also the not-inconsiderable cost of putting all our furniture into storage.

It was a problem. Not enough to stop us going ahead, but I couldn't shake the feeling that we didn't have sufficient contingency.

We spoke to our next door neighbour, a young man involved in the property business, with a view to getting his opinion on the best thing to do; and in the hope that we'd be able to get him to manage the letting on our behalf. Except that as soon as we told him what we were doing he said he and his partner would like to buy the flat off us.

It was a bit of a shock. This had never been part of the original plan, not least because nothing was selling in Edinburgh. This was knocking away every support and fallback position. We'd bought very late, at the top of the housing market, and if we cut our losses now the chances of us being able to buy anywhere in the future were remote.

Yet when I punched the new figures into the spreadsheet, it became obvious. We'd gain another pot of cash and massively reduce our outgoings. It would give us a degree of comfort. If we couldn't find work in Venice, we would at least have the chance to start again elsewhere.

There was really no decision to be made. We haggled a bit over the price, but, realistically, it was the only thing to do. In the middle of a desperate crisis in the housing market, we had been lucky.

That just left the question of what to do with all our possessions. We'd moved from a spacious rented property into a flat half the size and a third more expensive, for the dubious privilege of being able to say that it was 'ours'. As a result of this we'd already downsized significantly and got rid of a lot of our stuff. I'd taken so many boxes of old VHS tapes to the Oxfam shop in Morningside that they'd been able to hold a special SF and Horror video sale.

But we still had far, far too much and the cost of storing it all was going to be enormous. Then, on a weekend visit, my cousin happened to mention that they had some outbuildings that we could use. Well, this was marvellous, but it wouldn't seem fair to take advantage of this for free, surely? No problems, she said, her younger daughter was about to start university and would need a car. For obvious reasons, we weren't going to need ours in Venice; so they'd take the car off our hands and we could store all our possessions with them. OK, we'd have to transport everything down to their house in the New Forest, but it was still a good deal.

We'd been lucky again. The whole project was starting to seem like destiny. Caroline ended up working a ten-month period of redundancy, but was free to work on The Project full time from October 2011.

All I had to do now was successfully lose my job. I'd been assigned to a series of dead-end projects throughout the year, all of which were cancelled within months of initiation. I thought this had to be a good sign. Surely, if they couldn't find me any work to do during the most intense period of IT activity in years, they'd be more than happy to let me go. Surely I wouldn't suddenly become indispensable? Nevertheless, the thought was costing me more than a few sleepless nights. We needed to get lucky one more time.

Judgement Day

My manager sat across the table from me and laid out a sheaf of papers.

'This bit has to be formal, Phil, as you know'.

I half-nodded. I didn't trust myself to speak.

'I'm pleased to say your application for voluntary redundancy has been accepted.'

I let out a deep sigh. I might have cracked a watery smile, but my main recollection is of trying not to shake. She pushed a sheet of paper towards me.

'This is what we can offer you.'

I read it through. Almost exactly as I expected. The figure on the bottom line was not a huge one by any means. Yet again, I ran through the sums in my head.

'You don't have to sign it now. Talk to Caroline first if you like. But if you do sign, you have to be aware that this is final. You won't be able to change your mind.'

And for a few seconds I paused. I was certain, so absolutely certain that I wanted this. I had been almost sick with worry that morning, drinking endless coffees and cursing the fact that the consolation of a cigarette break was denied me. But, for a moment, I stopped and wondered. If I signed this, everything would change. Everything we'd managed to save over the past few years would be put at risk. There was no certainty that this would work. And if it failed, we would not be struggling IT professionals. We would be bankrupt ex-IT professionals, with worthless pensions, facing a bleak future.

The feeling lasted for a few seconds at most. Then the doubt passed and I reached for a pen. My breathing returned to normal, my heartbeat slowed.

'Are you quite sure, Phil?'

My hand was steady enough now and I scrawled my signature. I passed the forms back and slumped in my chair, exhaling heavily.

'Thank you. Really, thank you.'

She smiled. 'I'm glad you're pleased. We'll miss you. Are you off to tell Caroline then?'

'In a minute. I need a coffee first. Actually I need a drink, but a coffee will do for now.'

I got to my feet, somewhat unsteadily, and we shook hands.

I grabbed a coffee and walked back to my desk. At this time on Friday, most of my colleagues had left for the weekend. Only a few people around, and nobody gave me so much as a quizzical glance. I reached for the phone...

It was settled now. We really were going.

Se Non Ora, Quando?

Reaction to our news was mixed. Most people thought it was fantastic. The support we received was touching, and humbling.

There were, of course, a few Jeremiahs. It would have been strange if there hadn't been. There were understandable voices of concern along the lines of 'you'll find it difficult to get work' (fair point, there was no guarantee of this at all) which we accepted were well-meant; but also some rather strange ones.

'Is Caroline OK with this?' (No, I've made her give up her job and sold the house against her wishes).

'Are you Catholic?' (and, on being told no, 'Hmmm. It would be better if you were').

21

'But Italy is broken!' (Damn, now we've got no jobs and no home, why didn't you tell us earlier?)

I'd been reading the Italian papers for a couple of years, but by the end of 2011 you'd have had to have had your head in the sand to not realise what was happening. I became very familiar with the phrases *lo Spread vola* and *Borsa crolla*. There was no getting away from it, Italy had (and has) serious economic problems.

But what were we to do? Of course we would have felt better if we were leaving for a country with a booming economy, low unemployment and a prosperous population all desperate to spend some of their money on English lessons. But, in the middle of the worst economic crisis of my lifetime, this didn't seem likely in the near future.

No, it had to be now. Oh yes, we'd often hoped to be able to move to Italy in the future, but could we realistically plan for it? Could we assume we'd have our health? What's more, given the state of our pensions, there was no guarantee of being able to retire at all. And if we were moving to a country facing great uncertainties, we were also leaving a deeply unhappy one.

The chances of this opportunity coming along again seemed vanishingly small. It had to be now. *Carpe Diem*, or, if you prefer, *se non ora, quando?*

Part 2

Relocation

I have always been the dreamer in our relationship, Caroline the practical one. If there's a problem to overcome, I'm the one who thinks we'll always be able to improvise a way out of it, or that it'll just sort itself out in its own good time. Caroline is the strategist, the planner who leaves absolutely nothing to chance. If I had the vision, or the view from a hill, the whole project needed her forensic eye to ensure it had any chance of success. We'd read too many accounts of expat adventures, of people following 'The Dream', that had ended in unhappiness or financial disaster. If we were to succeed, we needed both of us to bring our individual strengths to bear.

She produced a twenty page document detailing every aspect of the Project in minute detail. It started with 'Get MOT for car' and ended with an exhaustive list of potential employers. Along the way, it took in accommodation, tax issues, health cover, residency and language. Every week had a list of issues that needed to be dealt with and crossed off before we could move on to the next stage. There was nothing it didn't cover.

We swithered over how much time it would take us to find long-term accommodation in Venice. We thought one week would be sufficient, but decided that two would give us just that little bit of contingency. With that in mind, we booked ourselves into a holiday flat we'd previously stayed at in Dorsoduro.

A date was fixed for the 3rd March 2012 and one-way flights were booked to Venice. This gave us approximately three months to complete the sale of the flat, move all our possessions into storage at my cousin's house and to retrain as English teachers.

It seemed a more than reasonable amount of time...

Independence Day

Birmingham, they say, has more canals than Venice. Edinburgh, almost certainly, has more roadworks than Naples. Sighthill is 7 miles from Leith and the rush hour drive takes 45 minutes. Every month, therefore, I spent 30 hours of my life inching my way to work, as the car bounced from pothole to pothole, along shoddy, badly-maintained roads. Every day I sat in traffic and imagined I could see the petrol gauge moving inexorably from right to left, burning up money for the most banal of purposes. And the reward for enduring this wretched journey was to arrive in work. It's a commute that brings out the worst in people. It brought out the worst in me.

On December 23rd, however, the streets were relatively clear as the city wound down for the festive season. The opening movement of Bach's Christmas Oratorio, the *Marseillaise* of Christmas music, played on Radio 3. I turned the volume up to maximum. *'Jauchzet! Frohlocket! Auf, Preiset die tage!'* - *'Rejoice, exult! Up, and praise the day!'* Oh yes, indeed, because this was my last day in work and I would never have to make this journey again.

Leaving a job - even one you hate - is never as much fun as you think it's going to be. God knows, I've left enough of them. Most of my friends had already finished for Christmas and my farewell email generated numerous 'out of office' messages, so my mood was downbeat. Cards, presents, much shaking of hands and good wishes. A final modestly boozy lunch with a handful of friends at a rather grim pub that people only ever seemed to go to for leaving drinks.

I'm not going to bang on about the evils of the banking industry. Your prejudices about it are probably correct. The prerequisite of a successful company is that it needs to be run for the benefit of customers, employees and shareholders. LBG, manifestly, was not working for any of them. If it were a football team, fans would have started chanting 'You don't know what you're doing' some time ago. But that wasn't the point. The job might have been horrible, but the people were a good bunch. Nice people who deserved better than this.

Time to go. I slipped my presents and my Swansea City mug into a box, and left the office for the last time.

My Swansea City mug was over twenty years old and had stayed with me since my student days, travelling with me through Holland, Germany, Switzerland, Italy and Scotland. Two hours later the bag containing my presents tore through and dropped a bottle of wine on top of it, cracking it irreparably. It felt as symbolic as Prospero breaking his staff.

There was no time to celebrate being out of work. The very next day we drove down to South Wales to spend Christmas with my parents for the first time in years. We arrived back to find a letter from our solicitor stating that missives were concluded and we had now, effectively, sold our flat.

We'd not been the best of home owners. I ignored a slowly-dripping tap for three years, until the day when it stubbornly refused to turn off at all. Over Christmas. A broken light socket with an exposed live wire a few inches above head height remained in place for a good eighteen months. The task of affixing pigeon spikes - necessitating balancing on a chair, on a narrow balcony, 60 feet above the ground - was one I entrusted to my 70 year old father. I have never been the most practical of men.

We had well and truly burned our boats now. If we were planning on coming back, it would have made sense to hang on to the flat, even though we'd make a loss on renting it out. However, we'd also decided that - should The Project fail - we probably wouldn't return to Edinburgh. It had been twenty years and it felt like time to move on.

We hoped that, at a stroke, the sale would remove all sorts of work and potential difficulties from Caroline's project plan. It was dispiriting to find out that the net effect was to shorten a twenty page document by a single side. Nevertheless, it simplified things somewhat and added a decent sum to the war chest. Burning boats, we thought, had worked just fine for Cortés .

Downsizing

In 1990, I considered Gary Moore's 'Still got the blues' to be the greatest rock guitar album of all time. I hadn't played a single track from it since 1992. And yet, I could hardly bear to get rid of it. Twenty years ago it was important to me. If it went, a little of my past would go with it. And this applied to hundreds of CDs, hundreds of books.

We needed to downsize and downsize considerably. Everything in the flat could be mentally labelled as Stuff We Needed, Stuff We Might Need In The Future and Stuff To Be Got Rid Of. Furniture could be similarly described as Sell or Store.

We undertook a purge of all our books. Classics which were available free as ebooks could go to the charity shop. Then there were those which we'd never got round to reading and probably never would; and those which, realistically, were never going to be read again. There were shelves of cookery books, far too many of which were used for a single recipe and nothing else. A signed copy of Sophie Grigson's 'Organic' failed to make the cut, on the grounds of never having been used at all. John Burton-Race's 'French Leave', also signed but never used, was similarly discarded; mainly because he'd managed to be rude to Caroline at the actual signing.

I came across Roger Protz's '300 Beers You Must Try Before You Die'. I think it may have been a fortieth birthday present. A quick flick through revealed a solitary Italian brew, *Nastro Azzurro*, a gardening beer best described as 'mostly harmless'. There wasn't going to be much need for it in Venice. Not without some regret, I put it on the discard pile

Clearing out my wardrobe revealed my old motorcycle jacket and helmet, kept for nostalgic reasons long after I'd got rid of the bike. It was time for them to go. I was delighted to find a very smart Paul Smith shirt, in immaculate condition, but – upon trying it on – I was disappointed to find that it appeared to have shrunk dramatically over the years. A black patterned shirt with silver buttons and collar tips reminded me of a time when I thought dressing like a dodgy country and western singer was a pretty sharp look for an evening out. A period of my life coincidentally known as 'The Single Years'.

We'd also managed to accumulate a substantial number of paintings. Nothing, unfortunately, that was likely to make us a huge amount of money if sold; but things that we liked, or just happened to be important to us. Most of these would need to be stored. Once they'd been taken down, the walls of the flat looked like somebody had gone berserk with a nail gun. The future owners, we hoped, would understand. And then there were those works that we seemed to have bought by mistake, that had never even been hung up, that could go directly to the charity shops.

A nice German lady bought half a dozen Ikea 'Billy' bookcases off us. I couldn't remember how the hell the removal men managed to get them upstairs in the first place, and so each and every one had to be taken apart in order to get them into the lift. Still, at least it was working for once; and nice German lady came prepared with an electric screwdriver. As a result, the spare room became a sea of orphaned books. Why, if we had got rid of so much, did it now look as if we had more than we had in the first place?

New Year
I've never liked New Year. As a kid, it means only one thing: Christmas is over, back to school. As an adult, it's even worse - you're going back to work and probably starting the year with a hangover as well. Lights and decorations come down, and we return to the cold, the dark and the rain until Spring. Or, if you happen to live in Edinburgh, we just return to the cold, the dark

and the rain.

Our previous Hogmanay had been a miserable one. I recalled standing on our balcony and watching the final trails of the fireworks at midnight; reflecting on a year blighted by family illness and the fear of losing our jobs. 2011 hadn't promised any better. Yet another year was starting with the threat of unemployment hanging over us. I don't mind playing games, but you can never hope to win against people who can change the rules whenever they feel like it.

Twelve months had passed. It turned out that there had always been a way to win and that was just to refuse to play. Yes, there were still things we couldn't do anything about, but for the first time in years, we were entering the New Year feeling happy and excited about the months ahead. We were in control of events instead of at their mercy and everything seemed possible.

We passed a pleasant Hogmanay with friends. Strong Drink was consumed in modest quantities. We got home at a sensible time, and I went to bed with a nice cup of tea and an improving book. Next morning we woke up, hangover-free, ready for the day and year ahead, and congratulated ourselves for being middle-aged.

The holidays, even in Scotland were now officially over. I had things of varying degrees of importance to crack on with: the essential (pre-course TEFL exercises), the fun (surfing for flats in Venice and seeing what was on at the opera) and the tedious-but-really-needed-to-be-done (arranging van hire).

So I set to the TEFL prep. To my chagrin it seemed to demonstrate that I did not actually have the ability to speak English at all. Still, there were five days left until the course started and I felt I could sort that out by then. Nevertheless, a vague melancholy was settling over me and I couldn't understand why. A general feeling of discontent, an unsettling anxiety that I was unable to shake. I really didn't know what to do with myself, so I pottered about brewing cups of tea, stared outside at a veritable hurricane blowing through Leith, grumpily channel surfed between Radios 3 and 4, and generally got under Caroline's feet.

And then it hit me. It was the day that I would normally be back at work. Subconsciously I was expecting to be in the office and I was feeling guilty about not being there. I'd only been at the bank for seven-and-a-half years and spent seven of those complaining about it; yet I was worried that the global financial system would go into meltdown if I wasn't there to personally sort it out. I put my TEFL exercises down. Van hire would have to wait until tomorrow. I logged on to the *La Fenice* website instead.

The Chalkface

I graduated over twenty years ago, but every few months or so I still get nightmares like this :

It's the end of my final year. I have been to no lectures at all. I have completed no assignments. I haven't done a scrap of work on my project. Today, my finals begin and I have done no revision. I am going to fail my exams and ruin the rest of my life...

I am frequently trouserless in these dreams as well, but that's another story for another time. I'd got away with it once and never again, I thought, would I have to formally study for any sort of qualification.

Except that now, of course, that's exactly what we both had to do. TEFL training started. And let no-one ever tell you that this is easy. You want me to stand up and deliver a lecture to a roomful of people? No problem. Would you like me to *sing* to a roomful of people? I'd be delighted. Hell, if Strong Drink had been consumed you'd have a job stopping me! But *teaching?* That suddenly seemed like another matter altogether.

After the first hour, I started to worry if I could do it.

After two hours, I was certain that I *couldn't* do it.

After three hours, the thought struck me that we had given up our jobs and sold our home and so we were bloody well going to *have* to find a way of doing it.

Still, neither of us had collapsed in uncontrollable tears after the first day, so that was a positive sign. We were yet to be let loose on actual, proper, money-paying foreign students. Perhaps they would be kind to us?

We were an eclectic bunch on the course. Two young women from Slovakia and Argentina whose knowledge of English grammar shamed the rest of us. A musician from Paris. A number of army personnel, there to improve their teaching skills prior to training members of the security forces back in Afghanistan. A man who had been attacked by a polar bear. We felt embarrassingly normal by comparison.

We had been warned about the amount of work that would be involved, but I had refused to believe it. How hard could it be? Yet I have never worked so hard in my life as I did during that month.

Upon returning home, I would prepare the most basic of meals, before hammering away at lesson plans and essays until the small hours. The television remained switched off. So did the radio. Our regular 'No Booze January' meant we were denied even the consolation of a restorative G&T. We lived an austere life of monastic asceticism.

But, in all honesty, I enjoyed that month enormously. It felt like having a proper, socially useful job at last. A job that I wouldn't be embarrassed to tell people about. I was genuinely excited by the thought of making a living from this.

We ate, slept and breathed TEFL for four exhausting weeks; and then we found ourselves with teaching certificates. OK, they were CELTAs and not PGCEs, but it had taken a lot of hard work to get that far.

For those who might be thinking about trying this: don't think that this is something you'll just be able to do. You won't. Don't think it's something that you can't fail. You can, and the experience of watching someone floundering in front of a class is a horrible one. Don't let anybody tell you it's 'not proper teaching'. It's proper teaching to those who are going to pay you money, and you owe it to them to treat it with a degree of seriousness and professionalism. Finally, clear your diary and make sure you do this during a quiet month. You cannot do this and maintain any vestige of a social life. Well you could, but I'm a grumpy old sod without my sleep and I'm far too old to be burning the candle at both ends any more.

It was a tough month but – completely against my expectations - one of the most rewarding things I'd ever done. It certainly changed my perspectives. Initially I'd just thought this would be a useful qualification to have in the event that I couldn't get a job doing anything else. By the end of it I found myself actively looking forward to putting it into practice. Maybe, all those years ago, I'd taken a wrong step with IT and this was something I should always have done.

It was sad to say goodbye to everyone on that final Friday night. They were a genuinely nice, interesting bunch of people, all there for very different reasons. We looked out for each other, supported each other and had a lot of laughs along the way. I wondered where we would all end up and if we would ever see each other again.

Everything now seemed very real and ominously close. We were to leave home in under a month's time. We had less than two weeks to pack. More importantly I still had nearly 2000 CDs to copy to my laptop.

Dial M for Mahler

'The eternal work is done' sings Wotan in *Das Rheingold*. This is commonly assumed to be a reference to the construction of Valhalla. I think it more likely that he'd simply been wasting the past centuries in a hopeless attempt to copy his record collection onto his PC.

Some things had to be given up. One example was the hi-fi and the racks of CDs. It wasn't practical to transport the whole lot to Venice and, realistically, we were not likely to be renting a place with sufficient space to store them all anyway.

Nevertheless, I did consider it possible that I could rip every last one of them to my laptop and have access to the whole lot. They might be in less-than-perfect quality sound, but it would be better than nothing.

Given that I had 2000-odd to convert and they all had to be packed away at least a month before the move, I should have given it about a year. Instead I left it until the final couple of weeks.

So compromises had to be made. What had to come with us? Beethoven, Brahms, Berlioz (actually, almost everyone that starts with a 'B'). As much Bach as physically possible. Everything by Wagner. Puccini. The Beatles, Jethro Tull and Hawkwind (oh, how our neighbours would love us). Caroline said she would divorce me if the Smiths and Morrissey didn't make the trip.

It was an interesting journey through my musical past. Philip Glass's *Einstein on the Beach*, in which a man basically chants *12341234123412341234* for two-and-a-half hours, made the cut. A set of ten austere string quartets by Peter Maxwell Davies might have repaid long term investigation, but there just wasn't time. Sorry Max.

And then there was Mahler. I had five different recordings of his sixth symphony. I couldn't remember buying them all. I wasn't at all convinced I'd listened to them all. And not only is it not my favourite symphony, it's not even my favourite *Mahler* symphony.

How had I ended up with five?

I'd made it as far as 'M'. The end was nowhere in sight and, right at the end, Wagner awaited, where rows upon rows of CDs and box sets and multiple recordings stretched into the distance like the rainbow bridge to Valhalla.

It was going to be a long week.

Morrissey did not make the trip. Caroline did not divorce me. Spotify and Youtube saved our marriage.

Cooking doesn't get tougher than this...

Pellegrino Artusi was a 19th century Florentine gentleman, famous today for his work *'La scienza in cucina e l'arte di mangiare bene' (The Science of Cooking and the Art of Eating Well)*. Written within 20 years of the unification of Italy, he is sometimes credited with establishing a national Italian cuisine. The Italian Cultural Institute in Edinburgh held a cookery competition to mark the centenary of his death and celebrate the re-publication of his great work. I thought I could take a bit of time off from working on the Project to have some fun.

The rules were that all dishes would be taken from Artusi's book, be cooked in advance and be judged on the night of the Institute's celebratory party. Now, this presented some obvious problems: namely that hot dishes wouldn't be practical and anything prepared needed to be capable of being transported, by bus, over the rattly old streets of Edinburgh and still look vaguely appetising by the end of the journey.

Pastries and desserts have never really been my thing, so this narrowed my options even more. There were always *crostini*, of course but...well, come now, *crostini* are more assembling than cooking, surely? No-one was going to win a cookery competition with *crostini*.

So I decided on Artusi's *Pane di Fegato*. Literally, a 'liver bread', part meat loaf, part *pate*.

I chopped up some calf's liver and gently fried it in a not-insubstantial amount of butter. I added some chicken livers, a healthy slug of Marsala and more butter. I seasoned with salt and pepper, and added breadcrumbs to absorb the juices.

I blitzed the mixture to a fine texture in the food processor. I then added some eggs, parmesan, stock and a little more marsala; re-checked the seasoning and tipped the whole lot into a loaf tin where I cooked it in a *bain-marie* for approximately 45 minutes before turning it out.

I took an organic chicken carcass, covered it with water, and simmered it for two hours, before reducing down the resulting stock to an intensely flavoured broth. Once cooled, I put it in the fridge for a few hours until it began to solidify into aspic.

I added a glaze to the loaf and then took four thin slices from an orange and laid them on top, before finishing with another glaze.

I made it twice, to be absolutely sure of what I was doing. It took a hell of a long time and cost a packet, but it was worth every minute. The texture was light and crumbly, the flavour surprisingly delicate. It looked utterly professional. It clearly demonstrated technical ability in any number of culinary skills.

The winner was a bloke who made *crostini*.

Saying Goodbye

Early one Tuesday evening. Caroline and I were treating ourselves to tea at *The Dogs* after another tough day. I had a rehearsal with the Edinburgh Bach Choir that same evening. Look, I said, I've got a ton of work to complete, I'm going to need every spare hour I can find and I could really do without going to practice tonight. And I realised I was making excuses, because it was going to be my last evening with them.

Of course Caroline persuaded me to go. I hadn't properly looked over my scores since Christmas - there hadn't been much time and, as I wasn't going to be able to make the next concert anyway, my heart hadn't been in it.

I hadn't planned to make any big announcement and thought I'd discreetly slip away after saying goodbye to those I knew best. It didn't work out that way. During the break our secretary stood up to read out the usual notices about rehearsals and upcoming concerts and, to my genuine surprise, added that *tonight we have some exciting but sad news, as Philip from the bass section is leaving us to move to Venice with his wife*. Applause, cries of surprise and I stood up to thank everyone. I would never get used to this sort of thing.

Handshakes, hugs and good wishes. Our conductor said they'd miss me and asked if there was any chance of arranging an exchange visit with a Venetian choir. I said I'd do my best to arrange the Monteverdi *Vespers* in St Mark's. I'm still not sure if he thought I was serious.

Caroline was already in bed when I got home. I gave her a hug and said I was going to sit up for a bit. I poured myself a large glass of wine, put a CD on and sat on the sofa and cried.

It was difficult saying goodbye to people and there was more, much more, of this to come. It never got any easier. But that was fine. Because this was never going to be a pain-free exercise. We both knew that we would have to give things up. We looked at what it would involve and still decided we wanted to do this. In a strange way, we found the seemingly never-ending round of goodbyes so draining and upsetting that it gave us confidence we were doing the right thing.

The choir wasn't a big enough thing in my life to put The Project on hold for. It was something that only occupied me for a couple of hours a week. But I had loved those years with them and enjoyed their company, and it saddened me that I wouldn't see them again.

The Biggest Casserole in the World

The Biggest Casserole in the World sat on a kitchen unit, silently mocking me as I stood there, helpless, in the face of its sheer immensity.

I hate packing.

I hate packing because I am rubbish at it. Caroline has quite the knack and packs things away with millimetric precision. I am not like that. I stared at the Biggest Casserole in the World in the manner of the ape creatures staring at the monolith at the start of Kubrick's *2001*.

'Do we really need this?'
'It's Le Creuset.'
'Yes, but we've never actually used it, have we?'
'I did, once. Before we met. It was the only thing that could hold a whole chicken.'
'So we've not used it since at least 1998 then?'
'No, but it was expensive. And it's Le Creuset.'

I was never going to win this one. I'd already got away with labelling one box as 'Misc. Chinese thingies' so I didn't feel like pushing my luck.

I felt akin to a riot policeman on the front line as I held the huge, circular lid out in front of me. I found a box of roughly the right size and packed it away. Never mind a whole chicken, this thing could have housed an entire free-range family. I taped it up, labelled it as 'Fragile' and then wondered why.

I manoeuvred it into position where it sat, tacitly asserting its authority over the other boxes of kitchen equipment. One day, oh yes, one day, I promised myself, we *would* cook the Biggest Chicken Casserole in the World.

Hell

If I ever meet the lovely man who designed the £25 trolley from B&Q, I will buy him a very, very large drink. Because, without his wonderful invention, I have no idea how we would ever have got the van packed in one day. As it was, it took the two of us seven hours. It was a disturbing thought that 95% of everything we owned was now sitting outside, overnight, in a convenient drive-away form. In Leith.

We went to the opera that night. Humperdinck's *Hansel und Gretel*, influenced by Wagner, but minus any of that Wagnerian *sturm und drang* and soul-searching. Or, indeed, length, which, at that moment, I was immensely grateful for. Conducting the premiere, Richard Strauss described it as 'a masterpiece of the first rank'. Richard Strauss, however, had not spent an entire day loading all his worldly possessions into a van and was not facing a 400 mile drive in the morning. All in all, this was one of those rare occasions when I was less than enthusiastic at the prospect of a night at the opera. Crawling into bed and sleeping for 12 hours seemed much the better option.

Many years ago, at primary school in South Wales, *Hansel und Gretel* was the very first operatic music I heard. There was, then, a pleasing symmetry to this being our last evening with Scottish Opera. It was a nostalgic evening to end on, with some fine playing and singing from a number of company stalwarts. Again, though, it was saying goodbye and it wasn't getting any easier.

After a very long, but blessedly uneventful, drive we arrived in the New Forest and by midday on Saturday I was standing in the middle of a near-empty van. The boxes had all been cleared and were ready to go up to the loft. Pretty much all that remained was to move the furniture into one of the outbuildings and we would be done. With five of us working we were already nearly finished, and it'd only been an hour. It was a fine, sunny day - rain was forecast for the afternoon but by that time, I thought, we'd be enjoying a late lunch in the pub.

Those blessed few minutes of delusion would prove to be the high point of the day.

The outbuilding itself was hidden away at the back of a large garden, concealed by trees and bushes. You sort of stumbled across it in a similar way to the last few minutes of 'The Blair Witch Project'.

We opened the door and looked inside. It was, not to put too fine a point on it, absolutely full of stuff. We had two chests of drawers, a large wooden table, a quadruple wardrobe and a bed frame in the van. This wasn't just a case of moving a few things out of the way – there was no way in hell we were going to fit everything in.

So a plan was needed. Cathy, Caroline and Zoe would clear out all the rubbish. Paul and I would bring the furniture down. Then, when the van was cleared, we'd chuck all the junk in the back and drive it to the dump. As we carried a wardrobe through a forest, in the rain, I began to suspect that the pub was not in our immediate future.

Eventually, we cleared the van and managed to squeeze the furniture into the shed. Paul and I retired to the kitchen to put the kettle on. Uncle Colin arrived to offer moral support and, after tea and a biscuit, things no longer seemed so bad. I wandered outside to see how the girls were getting on...

Somehow, I managed to maintain my grip on my cup of tea. The van, near-empty fifteen minutes ago, was jam-packed full of crap; full to the brim with cardboard boxes, tins of paint, flower pots, sheets of plastic, bicycles, scooters, garden furniture, a bed, a cooker hood and half of something which might once have been a *chaise longue*. There was not an inch of space left in there. In the space of 36 hours we had packed the van, unpacked it and now we were going to have to drive it to a dump and unload it all over again.

Cathy came over to me, saw the expression in my eyes, and looked genuinely concerned.

'Are you OK with this Phil? Really?'

I gulped, and tried to keep the hysteria out of my voice. 'Hey, it's a van full of shite Cathy, why wouldn't I be OK with it?'

I checked my watch. We had an hour and twenty minutes until the dump closed. Paul and I hauled our weary bodies into the van and set off.

I'd been living in hope that this was going to be a landfill and we could just shovel out the contents and head off again. Oh no. This was one of those facilities with a separate skip for every conceivable type of waste. I picked up a random, soggy cardboard box and made my way towards one marked 'Household Waste' when a Polish gentleman in a waxed jacket stopped me, examined the contents and informed me 'Electrical cable – metals – over there on left. Tins of paint – paint recycling opposite. Plant pots – household waste. Cardboard box – papers – over there. Plastics – next to cardboard'. Half-dazed, I stumbled from skip to skip. Another worker at the paints recycling bin sent me away for bringing the wrong type of paint.

Paul's face wore the haunted expression of a man who had taken a day off work in order to help us out, and who had realised that this wouldn't be happening to him if he'd just pretended his boss wouldn't give him the time off.

I grabbed a Fison's bag full to the brim with tins of paint that looked as if they might be special enough for the special paints bin. I dragged it over, opened the lid and tipped the whole lot in, realising too late that the bag was also half full of peat. I closed the lid in a hurry and beat a hasty retreat.

At this point we had a stroke of luck as the Polish chap abandoned his post, either to go for a cup of tea, or to avoid the sight of two grown men crying. We seized the opportunity of the 'Household Waste' bin being at our mercy and, with Herculean effort, the Van Full of Shite was cleared. We jumped in and headed for home before he could return to identify any rogue elements in his skip.

In our absence the girls had stashed away our paintings in a secure, concealed cellar (a nice touch, even if it did bring to mind images of fleeing Nazi war criminals). That just left one final push – forty-odd boxes needed to be taken up to the attic. We evolved an efficient production-line system: Cathy would drag a box from the pile and pass it on to me. I would push it up the ladder to Zoe, who would haul it through the gap and slide it on to Caroline and then on to Paul (who was the only one who knew which areas of the floor were load bearing and which areas would allow a box full of Swansea City football programmes to crash through with lethal force onto the occupants of the room below).

And then we were done. It felt like we should open a bottle of champagne but none of us would have had the strength to get the top off. It had been a bugger of a tough day, but nobody had fallen out, or been reduced to tears. As we relaxed over fish and chips and a modest amount of wine, I reflected that everybody had got something out of this. We had our free storage. Zoe had the car. Paul had two more guitars to play with. And Cathy...?

Cathy had the Biggest Casserole in the World!

The Cocktail Cardboard Box

There were now just three days to go before leaving Edinburgh. The flat was not quite an empty shell, but felt cold and depressing. A small spray of flowers in a mug sat atop an upturned plastic crate that served as a coffee table. We were sleeping on an inflatable mattress and cooking was reduced to whatever could be warmed up in the oven or microwave as we had no pans left. Laughing at the Biggest Casserole in the World no longer seemed so funny.

It wasn't all Dickensian deprivation and misery, however. We still had a lot of wine left which needed to be drunk before leaving. And then there was the strange case of the Cocktail

Cabinet, or, strictly speaking, the Cocktail Cardboard Box; a nostalgic look back at our drinking history. A tiny swirl of green fluid in a bottle was a reminder of the short-lived, and possibly ill-advised, absinthe revival of the late 1990s. There was a half glass of Pimm's left, as there had been since 1998. I had vague memories of cooking with kirsch and Strega; mainly because I couldn't imagine drinking either of them. And then there was a bottle of ouzo. Neither of us likes ouzo. I hadn't touched the stuff since a party in Swansea in 1988. Yet there was a near-full bottle of it that neither of us could remember buying. What was it doing there? Loath though we were to dispose of anything vaguely alcoholic and not actually poisonous, it went down the sink.

The Move

I sound more Welsh when I'm angry and I stood at the foreign exchange desk in Sainsbury's sounding Very Welsh Indeed. Not quite Bryn Terfel at the Millennium Stadium, more Neil Kinnock at the 1985 Labour Party conference, but the Welshometer was creeping into the red. I'd driven 40 minutes across town to pick up some euros and now the young man in the booth was telling me that my payment hadn't cleared and he couldn't give me anything. I told him I'd rung only an hour previously to check and had been told everything was ready. He apologised, but he couldn't do anything. I drove home. The moment I stepped through the door the phone rang. It was, of course, Sainsbury's. Everything was cleared now. I drove all the way back. The boy handed over my euros, without apology. I wasn't in a mood to accept one anyway.

This had wasted a whole morning when we had no time to waste. By now it was obvious that we'd massively underestimated the amount of work left. A hell of a lot of stuff still remained to be taken to the dump or to the charity shop, the place needed a good clean and we ('we' in this case meaning 'Caroline', as I'm really not to be trusted with things like this) hadn't even been able to start packing yet.

I spent the afternoon vacuuming and cleaning floors. I cleaned the windows. I then turned my attention to the oven. It hadn't been cleaned since before Christmas and the interior resembled something from *The Quatermass Experiment*. I attacked it with a noxious chemical goo, emblazoned with all sorts of dire warnings, which rendered down the unpleasantness into a thick, fatty black sludge. I knew there would be times when the glamour and excitement of The Project would fade. This was one of them.

Then it was time for our final Italian class, following which everyone headed off for a bite to eat and a few glasses of wine. It was our final big farewell do and bittersweet as always.

We returned home, feeling happier about things. The boys next door had bought us a very nice bottle of Riesling as a moving out present and we thought a glass or two before bed would be just the thing. Caroline went to check her email, just in case there was something that needed to be looked at urgently.

There was a message from the owner of the flat we were to be renting in Italy. The harsh Venetian winter had caused the pipes to burst in the flat upstairs from ours and, as a result of the flooding, it was in no fit state to be rented out.

It was just four days until we flew out and we no longer had a place to stay.

Caroline got up at 2:30 in order to start packing. I was going to need a proper night's sleep if I was to drive for seven hours so she let me sleep on, but I passed an uneasy night nevertheless.

There was no time to think about the flat, or lack of one, in Venice. Caroline packed and repacked, then repacked again. I shuttled back and forth, taking stuff down to the car for a final run to the charity shop, or just to throw directly into the building's communal bins. I completely filled one and half of the other, and started to worry if I might actually be done for tipping. *How* could there still be so much left?

I came across a small box containing a cuckoo clock, a

Christmas present I bought for my late grandmother whilst I was working in Switzerland. She loved it. And yet, I was never likely to hang a cuckoo clock on my wall. It broke my heart, but it had to go.

Everything seemed that little bit more difficult than it ought to have been. I had a bag full of kitchen knives. Charity shops, in Leith at least, do not take bags full of knives, and I'd been told to take them to the police station. So along I went, pressed the intercom and informed them that I was standing outside with a bag of knives that I'd like them to dispose of. Two young policemen came out. They seemed confused. I (slowly) held up the bag, through which sharp objects were already ripping holes, and explained the situation. They told me that they only disposed of actual weapons and these didn't count. I pointed out a wicked six-inch blade that, I imagined, might be used quite successfully as a weapon, but no – it wasn't a samurai sword or a machete, so they wouldn't take it. One of them tried to be helpful and told me that I should take them to recycling or even just put them in the bin. I looked around me. A skip was conveniently, enticingly, placed on the street only twenty yards away. It was enormously tempting. I shook my head. I was *not* putting a bag of knives into a skip in Leith. I drove out to the recycling depot, chucked them in the metals bin and then back home again.

Caroline was still repacking, but we could see an end to it now. Slowly, but surely, I loaded the car. Amazingly, everything that now met the definition of essential fitted. Every square inch of free space was used. Not a chink of light could be seen in the rear view mirror. Technically, I thought, this counted as overloading. It almost certainly wasn't very safe. If I had to do an emergency stop, Peter Howson's painting 'Figure kneeling in graveyard' was likely to hurtle forward and decapitate me.

We should have left the flat at 10:00. It was now 2:00 in the afternoon. Caroline had been working, non-stop, for twelve hours. I now needed to drive to Sheffield for the first stop on our farewell tour. Both of us were shattered. This had easily been the grimmest day so far but surely – *surely* – this had to be the worst over now?

'Let's go to Venice', I said, and we left Edinburgh, and Scotland, for perhaps the last time.

A few days later and our morale had improved no end, due to the company of friends and heroic quantities of wine. Even the situation with the flat had resolved itself as we'd been told that - while it would need redecorating at some point - it would still be in a fit state for us to move into. I had no idea what a 'fit state' meant, but I was past caring. If it had a roof, it would do.

Caroline repacked yet again and managed to reduce the number of cases to what we hoped would be a manageable number. Ten. I thought it was time for me to make the big gesture and told her that – if it would help at all – I was prepared to forego taking my opera cloak with me. She told me that it had failed to make the cut four days previously.

We were staying with my cousin Susie and her husband Justin who would be driving us to the airport. Cathy and Paul arrived to say cheerio and to pick up the car. I handed over the documentation and then suggested to Paul that I should run through some of its little quirks such as the non-cancelling indicators and the intermittently successful central locking. I showed him how the satnav worked and the travel computer.

'I can't help noticing', he said, 'that all the instructions seem to be in Italian.'

'Yes, I changed all the language settings a few years back. I thought it would be a good way to practise.'

'Right. Any idea how you switch them back?'

'Erm, I can't honestly remember. Sorry. Anyway, Zoe speaks Italian...doesn't she?'

'Well...I guess she's going to learn.'

Sue and Justin drove us to Gatwick in an efficiently packed and extremely snug, Zafira; and then it was final hugs and goodbyes. We watched their car disappear, hauled our bags onto trolleys and realised that we were now on our own.

Six months ago we had jobs, a flat and a car, and now we didn't even have any keys. If our luggage failed to arrive we'd be left with the clothes we were standing up in. The time to be nervous was long past. There wasn't even any apprehension now, just a sense of absolute freedom.

I tried to watch and remember every minute of the final approach to Marco Polo. It felt like coming home. It wasn't, of course, and the following months would show us how much we still had to learn; but I was aware that, whenever we made this flight in the future, it would never be quite the same, never quite as special as this occasion.

A water taxi from the airport to Venice was expensive but the only way to transport so much luggage in one go, and it was a special way to arrive. As the boat entered the Grand Canal, I imagined I was Lord Byron arriving in this great city for the first time. Byron probably didn't have a laptop case on his knee with a copy of Doctor Who Magazine poking out, but still. The driver dropped us off at Campo San Barnaba, which was the nearest we were able to get to our flat. It was only a few hundred yards away, but a few hundred yards with ten heavy bags between two of us was not going to be possible in one go, so Caroline headed off to get the keys while I watched the luggage. Giuseppe, the guy who looked after the flat, was out of town until later that evening, so he'd made arrangements to leave the keys with a Signor Colussi who lived a few doors down.

Caroline returned after fifteen minutes. Signor Colussi did not appear to be at home. Not to worry, we'd made good time and it was warm enough to sit outside, so we dragged our luggage to a nearby bar and ordered some drinks.

Time passed and I thought perhaps I should go and check what was going on. Signor Colussi did not answer his door, but his neighbour saw me ringing and informed me that she thought he was out of town at the moment.

Oh. Still, there was no reason to worry, Giuseppe would be back in the evening, I'd just give him a call on his *telefonino* and see what time he was due back.

There was no answer.

We ordered some more drinks, but it was starting to get chilly now and no longer felt like ice cold *Peroni* weather. We gave it another half hour and then Caroline remembered she had Giuseppe's address so she could at least go and bang on his door and see if he was back.

I sat there and drew my coat around myself. It was properly cold now and getting dark. I did not know of any hotels in the area and didn't know how we were going to be able to look for one whilst trying to cope with ten heavy bags. It would be fair to say that, by the time Caroline returned, I was in danger of working myself into A State.

Happily, she had found Mrs Giuseppe at home, where she had been all afternoon with a spare set of keys, and who thought it quite funny that we'd spent hours nursing our drinks in the cold when our nice warm flat was only a few hundred yards away.

It took three journeys to transport all our luggage. I hauled the last of the bags upstairs and looked around. There were a few areas where it was evident that paint had crumbled from the ceiling; but we'd finally made it. It was dry, it was warm and at that moment it was the best damn flat in the whole of Venice.

Part 3

Arrival

Nothing felt quite real in those first few weeks.

We quickly realised that we were not on holiday. On previous visits we had kidded ourselves that renting an apartment and cooking at home was the same as being a local. It was nothing like it, of course. Our first trip to the *Billa* supermarket on the Zattere brought it home. It's one thing shopping for food as a tourist. It's another thing entirely to try and find banal household staples – bleach, washing up liquid, kitchen towel, toilet rolls – when nothing is the same as back home; when you find yourself without the safety net of reassuring brand names, or the instinctive knowledge of what something should cost.

Everything was different. The radio was different. The television was different. The newspapers were different. Who the hell were all these people being referred to on the news anyway?

There was also the issue of language. Well-meaning Venetians noticed that our Italian was less than perfect and would, after initial pleasantries, speak to us in English. This led to strange and frustrating conversations where both parties would obstinately plough ahead in the other's native tongue, as if not wanting to admit defeat. And the trouble with this is that it made us feel like visitors, as if we didn't belong.

After the past few months, it would have been pleasant to relax a little, to just be on holiday for a while, but there was no time for this. We'd assumed two weeks would be plenty of time to find a long-term place to stay. Short-term rentals, even outside peak season, can be expensive and the clock had now started ticking. Quite simply, the longer we had to spend in a holiday apartment, the more money – money that we could ill-afford to waste – was burning up.

Yet for all that, there were those lovely moments of strolling through Dorsoduro and realising that we were not going home. We lived here now and had all the time in the world to enjoy it.

Day 1

Bits of ceiling plopped gently onto my head as I shaved. I looked up and noticed that another bit had crumbled away, and shook some paint and plaster fragments from my brush. The flat seemed nice enough at first glance but, if you raised your eyes from the horizontal, it became obvious that our landlady and Giuseppe were going to have more than a little redecoration to do.

There was work to be done and lots of it, but we felt we could spare one day off. It was a cold, blustery day, with the winter sun breaking through. Venice was quiet, a genuine pleasure to walk around. We bought some fish from a stall in Campo Santa Margherita, *merluzzi*. I had no idea what they were, but they sounded terribly exotic. Fish on a Tuesday was something of a luxury for us, the fishmongers of Sighthill being notable by their absence. We picked up some *vino sfuso*, a basic white wine, coming in at just under two euros a litre.

Home for lunch, and Caroline did some work on putting together a list of flats that might repay investigation. Then we strolled down from Dorsoduro to Piazza San Marco. There were a few lines of tourists but they seemed outnumbered by *extracomunitari* selling imitation Louis Vuitton bags, a few of whom were hurriedly packing their wares away, presumably at the approach of the police. Ten minutes later we indeed saw two policemen walking across the square, bearing a big pile of Mr Vuitton's not-quite-finest.

I baked the *merluzzi* (which turn out to be nothing more exotic than cod) for dinner, along with some *cima di rapa*. Washed down with some budget prosecco and some even-more-budget white wine, it all felt like a bit of a treat.

The Consolations of Risotto

Another piece of plaster dangled ominously from the ceiling, but I'd become a dab hand at this by now and positioned an empty pedal bin beneath, before gently prodding the offending piece so that it dropped into the waiting receptacle instead of crashing to the floor and fragmenting into a thousand pieces. I felt quietly pleased with myself, all the more so when we went to the fish market and managed to discuss the subtle, but important, differences between two species of clam without too much confusion.

Day 2, however, was a day of starting to grapple with red tape.

The Codice Fiscale is, supposedly, the easiest piece of documentation to acquire, and so it proved. We arrived at the *Azienda delle Entrate* and sat in a queue for ten minutes, until an affable gentleman checked our passports and gave us the required documents. All done and dusted, all conducted in Italian and he even chuckled politely at a feeble joke of mine. Frankly, we were wondering what all the fuss was about regarding Italian bureaucracy.

The Resident's Certificate was a different matter. We needed proof of our savings (we forgot to bring that), of our health cover (in the post) and a translation of our marriage certificate (hadn't even thought of that) although the more obliging of the two women in the office suggested that the last one wasn't really that important and we could just pretend to be living in sin if that made things easier. The less obliging of the two advised us to come back when we spoke Italian. Caroline at least had the presence of mind to ask them to write down everything we needed to bring along next time, on a post-it note. This would prove to be invaluable.

We found ourselves standing outside, shell-shocked. We'd thought we were properly prepared for everything and, all of a sudden, the most important things didn't seem to be possible at all. And it turned out we didn't really speak Italian.

This brought us back down to earth like, well, a piece of soggy plaster dropping from a bathroom ceiling. But the Joneses don't give up and have a little cry in times of adversity. No, they seek solace in Strong Drink; and in the company of a beer and a view of the Giudecca canal on a sunny day, few problems seemed insurmountable.

I cooked risotto with *vongole* for dinner, as a Maria Callas compilation played in the background. I don't even like Callas that much; nevertheless the whole experience felt stereotypically, but magnificently, Italian (*).

* Yes, I know she was Greek.

In Praise of Venetian Rabbits

You don't have to do anything in Venice. It is enough just to be there. The weekend allowed us time off from the job of settling in to wander around and enjoy the city. It had been sunny for days now, the skies a clear blue; still cold in the shade, but feeling like it would be just a few more weeks until it was jackets instead of coats.

We bought a rabbit from a butcher's in S.Margherita. He only had half of one left, but it must have been a fearsome beast in life. It would have been a brave fox that dared to meddle with it. Hell, I'd have been scared, looking at the size of the thing.

Vegetarian friends, please look away now. Nothing of interest remains in this section.

We weren't kitted out for doing any fancy cooking and neither did we want to be buying lots of ingredients. So here is the simplest of recipes for 'Rabbit Jonesy-style'.

It came complete with (half) its offal, so I warmed some oil in a pan, flipped out the half of the brain and gently fried it (veggie chums, if you're still here, I did warn you, and it doesn't get any better). I finely chopped the kidneys, liver and tongue, and added them to the pan. I turned up the heat, added the rabbit pieces, and fried them until golden and crisp on the outside. Then I added the juice and zest of half a lemon, a few sprigs of rosemary, a very healthy glug of white wine, and covered it for fifteen minutes.

Served with some *cavolo nero* and crusty bread, it was without doubt the tastiest rabbit dish I had ever cooked. It could easily have fed four; nevertheless we had no problems scoffing the lot and the bones made for a fine stock as well.

Flat-hunting started in earnest on Monday morning. We found an apartment we liked, decided it was 90% perfect and then dithered whilst we pondered whether we could live with the other 10%. Inevitably, by the time we decided to go for it, it had gone.

Later that same day we saw a small flat tucked away in Castello; not ideal in terms of size or location and we suspected it might be prone to *acqua alta* as well. It was reasonably priced, however, and – being on the ground floor - would at least allow for the acquisition of a small Venetian cat. That wasn't enough to make it a realistic possibility, but it was something to add to the list.

Dinner that evening was *Pasta alla Norma*, only made with Venetian *bigoli* instead of spaghetti. I'd like to say this was a deliberate attempt at Venetian/Sicilian fusion cuisine, but no. We just didn't have any spaghetti in the cupboard. Aubergines are happy to absorb as much olive oil as you care to throw at them (and I threw a *lot* at these) so it may not have been the healthiest of dishes, but, even though I say so myself, it was pretty good.

A visit to the Co-op in Cannaregio had introduced us to the 90 cent litre of wine. Previously we'd thought the *vino sfuso* concept (take along plastic bottle – chap behind counter fills it up from enormous vat for not-very-much-money-at-all) was as good as it got, but this was a whole step beyond. For 90 cents (or, in this case, 60, as there was a sale on) you took home a litre of wine in a Tetra Pak.

So how good could a 90 cent litre of wine be? The answer is that - whilst it was unlikely to win any awards - it was better than something that price had any right to be. It was one for drinking with food instead of knocking back in front of the television, but it really wasn't bad at all.

I leave you to ponder the likely social effects if the 90 cent litre of wine ever made it to the UK. In Leith, at least, they'd have to introduce Martial Law.

Giudecca

If Venice is a fish (and it is, just look at it on a map), then Giudecca is the curved sliver of land beneath the underbelly; separated from the main island by the Giudecca canal. It's not a part of Venice we know particularly well. We usually made a visit during Biennale time when the Welsh pavilion was housed in an ex-brewery here. Nowadays the brewery is being converted into luxury apartments, but one scuffed 'Cymru' sticker remains on the pavement as a reminder.

We were here to see a flat. This wasn't really the area we most wanted to stay in and the flat was in a modern development which wasn't ideal either, but it seemed worth checking out nevertheless. Rents are cheaper here, but on the downside we'd have an increase in commuting time as we'd need a boat to get anywhere we were likely to be working.

The flat itself was far better than we expected. Bigger than anywhere we'd seen so far (for that matter, it was bigger than anywhere we'd ever lived), it came complete with every mod con and an outside terrace on two sides. On one side it looked towards the island of *La Grazia,* on the other towards the church of the *Redentore.* It was a hell of a lot of flat for the money. Yet it wasn't quite right. The view towards the *Redentore* was a lovely one, but also interrupted by a number of uninspiring modern buildings. If – as we thought – we might only be able to stay for a year, then we needed to find somewhere exactly right.

Still, it was a possibility. It was a bright, sunny day but pleasantly cool in the quiet, shady streets; so we took a stroll around. Giudecca is home to a number of intriguingly abandoned churches: *Santi Cosma e Damiano* has been converted into that most banal of things, a 'business centre', which itself looks deserted. *Le Convertite* is a women's prison. The guidebooks can't seem to agree on what has become of *Santa Croce* – opinion is divided as to whether it's an old people's home or a prison. After being shouted at by some guards for daring to look inside the gates, we can now confirm to the world that it is, indeed, a prison. Either that, or it's the toughest old people's home you're ever likely to find.

With no plans for the afternoon, we headed back to Dorsoduro and took a long lunch outside on the balcony. The 90c bottle of wine had now been usurped by the 69c litre from *Billa*. 'Clever Vino Bianco' (for so it was called) was *just* about white wine flavour. But only just. It didn't need to be tried again.

A Short Move

I'd miscalculated how long it would take us to find a flat. I'd naively assumed we could sort it out within a week; two at the most. But we were finding that Italy didn't work like that. In addition, the more places we saw, the more our ideas were firming up as to the kind of place we really wanted. This meant somewhere in the *centro storico* proper and having somewhere to sit outside. Caroline had said this was non-negotiable. I could understand her position. We'd spent seven years in an apartment in Edinburgh with a balcony that was never used.

We were still in temporary accommodation, but had needed to move out of the flat in Calle Lunga. We would have stayed if the option had been there but the owner was no longer replying to our emails. In addition, I was starting to get tired of the increasing state of dilapidation. The ceiling, at least, seemed to have stabilised, but mould had started growing at an alarming rate on one of the walls and, whilst I didn't mind having to occasionally hoover up crumbling plasterwork, I drew the line at donning a biohazard suit and washing all the surfaces down with bleach.

The new place in San Basilio, by contrast, felt bright, airy and clean; and I thought the structurally sound ceiling compensated for the lack of a balcony.

We'd never really thought about living in San Marco and had hoped to find somewhere further from the madding crowd. Yet one of the properties we'd seen in the area looked absolutely perfect, almost enough to risk making an offer without even seeing it. We nevertheless disciplined ourselves to waiting a week until the owner was back in town.

We'd been warned that we should on no account be too enthusiastic when flat-hunting in Venice. People would always be willing to negotiate, indeed, they'd be expecting to. So that's what we intended. We'd be cool about it and express mild interest, but nothing more.

Our good intentions lasted the time it took to climb up to the *altana* and see the view that extended right over the *sestiere* of San Marco, past the *campanile* of Santo Stefano and over to the dome of the *Salute*. We looked at each other and nodded. We had to have this place. We'd just give the owner what she wanted. Hell, we'd give her more if need be. We tried not to babble too much as we spoke to her.

Dinner that night was Venetian-style calf's liver and onions, with a side dish of baked *radicchio*. The 69c 'Clever Vino Rosso' seemed better than the white but, given I was drinking this to celebrate the Welsh Grand Slam, I was in no position to give an objective opinion.

Stormy Monday

My mobile rang at 10:30 in the morning, sending me jumping a foot in the air. I checked the number and hastily stabbed the reply button. This could only be about the flat. We'd been fretting about it all weekend and were tetchy and on edge.

'Philip speaking...yes....yes...ok.'

Caroline, ashen-faced, leant on a kitchen unit for support.

'...ok...yes...right...'

Caroline made frantic, worried 'what *IS* it?' gestures at me.
'...ok...yes...I understand...yes...'
I gave her a thumbs-up.
WHEEEEEEEEEEEEEEEEEEEEEEEEEEEEHHHHHHHHH!!!!!
'...yes...yes, that was my wife...yes, she *is* pleased.'

Neither of us had really expected to get it but it seemed that the owner had, in principle, agreed.

That being the case, we needed to head down to the agency's office in San Marco to make a formal offer. It was a pleasant walk along the Zattere, despite the grey skies and light drizzle. Within minutes of turning into San Marco, however, the heavens opened with a great crack of thunder. It took only five minutes until one of my boots started leaking. After ten minutes, both of them were. As we crossed the bridge over to San Moisé we saw a mournful looking group of tourists in a gondola, putting a brave face on what must have been a bit of a dispiriting experience.

Water poured in torrents from the waterspouts around St Mark's Basilica; the piazza itself near-empty as people sheltered in the arcades. It struck us that we were in no great hurry and could make the most of the opportunity to just pop into the Basilica.

Think about that for a minute. How extraordinary, what a privilege, to be able to just 'pop into' St Mark's in the same way as one might drop by a bookshop or newsagent.

It is the most lovely of buildings and yet previous visits had always been disappointing; sadly shuffling around, shoulder-to-shoulder, in the midst of great throngs of visitors. There never seemed to be any space, or silence, to appreciate it properly. Yet on that afternoon - whether it was the time of year or the bad weather keeping people indoors – it was relatively quiet. In an ideal world I'd like the place to myself, to stretch out on the floor and gaze up at the ceilings. But, given that's unlikely to happen, this was one of our better experiences there.

On to the agency to sign the initial documentation, although we would still have to wait until the following Thursday for a formal agreement to be completed. Still, it had been a good day, and even squelching home in some very soggy socks failed to take the shine off it. I couldn't be bothered cooking so we headed off to *Al Profeta* for pizza. We even spent more than 69c on wine.

Signed and Sealed

A visit to the bank involved a walk along the Zattere and crossing the Grand Canal via the Accademia Bridge, leaving us time for a coffee in Campo Santo Stefano. Back in Edinburgh, it required a 45 minute drive from Leith to Sighthill. This took roughly the same amount of time but, as an experience, the similarities ended there.

Opening a bank account over here seems to be a relatively straightforward process, although simplified by a friend of ours who had very kindly telephoned her branch to tell them that two Brits would be arriving at some point. They seemed to have been expecting us, everyone was very helpful and polite and within twenty four hours we had an account and a bancomat card. You have to sign about a dozen different forms, but compared to the Byzantine complexity of opening, say, an Irish bank account (a tortuous saga that took me three months) this was a walk in the park.

Incidentally, before opening a bank account, you need an Italian mobile phone as they won't give you access to online banking without one. And you can't get a mobile, even pay-as-you-go, unless you have a *Codice Fiscale*. There is, probably, some good reason for this.

Bit by bit, we were knocking things off. We were now proud possessors of a flatteringly entitled 'Super Genius' account. I liked to think this ranked somewhere above the basic 'Quite Clever' account and that someday we might hope to upgrade to full 'Renaissance Man' status.

It took half the number of signatures to complete a year long lease on our flat. It had been a stressful week. Every time the phone rang we assumed it was the agency ringing to tell us that the owner had changed her mind. But, in an official ceremony at their office, it was all finally completed. Everything, again, was extremely formal in comparison to the UK. Sitting around four sides of a glass and chrome table in a modern office space, drinking miniscule espressos from chic little coffee cups, it felt akin to Reagan and Gorbachev signing the Reykjavik agreement.

There were a few more hoops to jump through. Our landlady (a perfectly nice woman, to be fair to her) was understandably nervous about renting her lovely flat to two unemployed Brits. Our workaround, and something I'd always thought might be our ace in the hole, was to offer the year's rent upfront. It *still* wasn't as easy as all that, as the process of transferring a large amount of money from a British account to an Italian one is laborious and difficult. I liked the idea of turning up at the final meeting in a sharp suit and dark glasses, with a briefcase full of euros chained to my wrist, but Mario Monti's new government had made any cash transaction above 1000 euros illegal. This time the solution was to transfer the entire amount, over two days, in 9 bite-sized chunks. Each one of those payments incurred a charge of nine quid. Banks. Don't we love them?

Still, it was hard to get wound up about it. Everything was signed, sealed and almost delivered. Within a week, the flat would be ours and we could start to believe that, yes, we really lived here.

The Patriarch

Venice is unique among Italian cities in being a Patriarchate, a distinction awarded to it in the 15th century in recognition of its power. These days, the title of *Patriarch* confers no particular privilege in itself, but nevertheless the position is a prestigious one - it supplied three Popes within the 20th century alone.

The seat became vacant when the incumbent Patriarch, Angelo

Scola, moved on to bigger and better things (Milan, that is, not Heaven). His replacement was Monsignor Francesco Moraglia, who was formally installed on March 25th 2012. Arriving by train, his cortege set off down the Grand Canal, stopping for prayers at the *Salute*, and then off to St Mark's to celebrate Mass for the Feast of the Annunciation.

Whatever your religious convictions may be, his arrival was a mightily impressive sight. Surrounded by gondolas and boats from seemingly every rowing club in the city, he was escorted by numerous police boats and outriders kitted out in helmets and body armour. Police outriders in Venice ride jet skis. I imagine that must be a fun job.

Bridges across the Grand Canal were temporarily shut (or at least the public were moved away from the bits directly above the Patriarch's gondola) and the canal had been closed to other traffic for the duration; although one *vaporetto* blithely continued on its way against the flow of the cortege, the driver cheerfully oblivious to the chorus of angry beeping from police boats and, indeed, to any potential threat to his immortal soul.

We had no trouble at all in finding a decent vantage point, which surprised us a little. It was even more surprising to find ourselves following His Beatitude into the half-empty *Salute*. We stayed to follow his investiture at St Mark's via the big screens installed in the church, and then - given that it seemed destined to go on for rather a long time - left just before the Mass began in earnest.

Yet despite all the colour and spectacle and the sense of being privileged to be there at a little moment of history, I couldn't help thinking that the streets and bridges seemed no busier than normal. The *Gazzettino* reported twenty thousand were at Piazza San Marco to welcome him. I can only say that the crowds looked considerably more modest to us. Times are changing, even in a city of over one hundred churches.

Fixed Abode

March 2012 is an odd month to look back on for all sorts of reasons; not the least of which is that, for four weeks, we really were of No Fixed Abode. And the Italians struggle with that concept. On numerous occasions we were asked to supply a permanent address and the typical response to being told that we didn't have one was a look of baffled incomprehension. In Italy, you *can't* not have a permanent place to live. It isn't possible. If you're trying this yourself, make sure you've got an address in your home country that you can use for this sort of thing.

Finally, the day of the Big Move arrived. The distance between our holiday flat in Dorsoduro and our apartment in San Marco was about half a mile, as the crow flies. But half a mile as the crow flies, in Venice, can easily turn into five miles. Ten, if I was navigating. Confusingly, it could also become *less* than half a mile. Venice is no respecter of the laws of Euclidean geometry.

The move involved transporting ten back-achingly heavy bags over a number of bridges. So any route chosen had to minimise these. It took patience, time and planning of near-military precision to work it out. Needless to say, I had no part in it. We hauled as many cases as we could manage to the San Basilio stop and took the *vaporetto* down to Zattere. Just one stop, but it cut out a bridge. Then we walked to Accademia and took the number one service to Sant Angelo. Then, after a short walk and a bridge of manageable dimensions, we were there. Straightforward enough and it only took three journeys. I still got lost twice.

No cooking was ever likely to happen that night. We enjoyed a pizza of modest quality and immodest price (ah yes, we were in San Marco now) before moving on for coffee and *grappa* at what turned out to be an excellent bar on the splendidly named *Rio Tera dei Assassini*.

So what started out as a 'blokes in pubs' conversation had become a pipe dream, then a fully-fledged Project and now - we'd done it.

Somehow, we'd actually done it. Yes, there was a huge amount of work still to do – health cover, residency, improving our Italian, *work* - but as we sat on the *altana* of our flat, watching the sun going down, the only thing that mattered was: we lived in Venice now.

Night of the Crabs

Moeche: Venetian soft-shell crabs so delicate they can be fried and eaten whole. Something of a delicacy these days, I'd only had them once before in my entire life. Caroline managed to buy a dozen at the market for a bargain seven euros.

These were going to be a bit of a challenge. You can't just chuck them in the frying pan. No, first you have to give them a good long soak in water in order to purge them. Now it's important that the little chaps are alive when you buy them, but these seemed totally inert. Nevertheless, immersion in the sink perked them up no end and some of the bigger ones were keen to explore the limits of their new environment. Perhaps a little too keen. I made sure I counted them all properly, just in case I returned in a few hours to find a couple had made a break for it. Oh yes, and if left alone for too long they'll start eating each other. I was worried I'd return and find a solitary really big crab sitting there contentedly.

Next step (vegetarian friends, you know the drill by now) is to beat a few eggs in a bowl, with a sprinkling of salt, and immerse our crustacean chums in the mix. The theory is that little crabs are absolutely bonkers for raw egg and will eat and eat and eat until (and the theories are divided on this) they either painlessly eat themselves to death, or just fall into a deep, deep sleep. At which point you dredge them in flour and into the pan they go.

Whatever the theory, I can honestly say that none of them were moving either before or after entering the pan, which was something of a relief as I wasn't relishing the idea of prodding any escapees back into the hot oil.

And were they worth it? With a healthy sprinkling of salt and lemon they were, without doubt, one of the most delicious things I've eaten. If you get the chance, try them.

A gondola passed by our flat that same evening. The gondolier was singing *O Sole Mio*. Seriously. It's not even a Venetian song (at least one *Lega Nord* politician has got very cross about this sort of thing) but, come on, we'd been in the flat for just a week and now a gondolier had floated past singing *O Sole Mio*. There may be a more archetypically Venetian experience but – short of finding oneself following a sinister red-cloaked dwarf through the foggy streets – I struggle to think of one.

We were settling in now, and finally unpacked, after what seemed like months of living out of suitcases.

It was interesting to see what had made the trip and what hadn't. I had arrived with two dress shirts, a bow tie, a selection of cufflinks and a white silk scarf. I would have looked quite the chap about town but for the fact that the accompanying dinner suit was back in the UK. Poignantly, I had the detachable pocket from my opera cloak, but not the actual cloak itself. The camera, we could only assume, was somewhere in Hampshire. Yet, strangely, my ancient Swansea City scarf had made it. It had enormous sentimental value (I explained to Caroline that it was at Preston in 1981, but that didn't have the expected impact) but it wasn't something I'd actually *worn* in over thirty years.

A shame about the camera, but the extra scarf, I thought might be handy come the winter.

Stabat Mater

Giovanni Battista Pergolesi is one of those composers who is only popularly remembered for a single iconic work. His *Stabat Mater*, commissioned as a piece for Good Friday in honour of the Virgin Mary, was written early in 1736. Admired greatly by, among others, JS Bach, it proved enduringly popular. Pergolesi never lived to enjoy its success. Within weeks of its completion, he was dead of tuberculosis. He was 26 years old.

A performance of his great work was held at the church of the *Salute*, on the Thursday before Holy Week. The *Santa Maria della Salute*, to give it its full name, is one of Venice's 'Plague Churches'. It was commissioned as a plea for deliverance from the pestilence of 1630-31 that would ultimately kill a third of the city's population. The architect chosen was the 26 year old Baldassare Longhena, but buildings like this don't just get thrown up overnight, and he died at the ripe old age of 82, five years before the building's consecration.

I like the *Salute*. In contrast with its Venetian Baroque exterior, the octagonal interior feels clean, unfussy and spacious. There was a modest audience for the performance (a number of people dropped by for a quick pray and then went on their way) but it was a good one. The two singers were almost concealed, high up in the organ loft behind Longhena's great Baroque altar. As a result, the opening phrase *Stabat Mater Dolorosa* seemed to emerge from nowhere, to echo around the apse. Spine-tingling music and a fine way to spend the afternoon.

That evening we fixed our nameplate over our doorbell. It felt as it we should have cracked a bottle of Prosecco over it.

Holy Week

Twenty years have passed since my first experience of living and working in Italy. In 1994, I spent six months in Monteporzio Catone, a small town in the Alban Hills outside Rome. One evening, I became aware of a lot of noise coming from the square behind my flat; so I stuck my head out of the window to see what was going on. It turned out to be a fully-fledged Passion Play; complete with a convincingly bloodied Christ dragging his cross through the streets, followed by a sizeable number of the residents. With eerie - and suitably apocalyptic - timing, the skies darkened, a colossal storm broke, and within minutes the streets were awash and lights flickered on and off throughout the town.

With every passing year, Easter, in the UK at least, seems to be becoming little more than just another Bank Holiday. It feels different over here. There's the sense that it still matters to people.

With that in mind, we decided to attend Mass at St Mark's on the Thursday night. I have to say that I really wasn't convinced this was a good idea. Neither Caroline nor myself are Catholic, so was this not – at best – disrespectful? Indeed, I was half expecting to be turned away at the side-entrance to the Basilica (I have no idea why I thought this, perhaps I imagined we'd have to complete some sort of theological questionnaire to be allowed in). The church, however, is properly geared up for this sort of thing. The most significant parts of the Mass are prefaced by translations in four languages and it is stressed that only Roman Catholics should receive Communion. And, crowded though the Basilica was, it was evident that more people could have fitted in – it wasn't as if we were denying one of the locals a place.

We managed to follow things reasonably well (it's not all that different from the Anglican service), considering that we were constantly having to mentally leap between Latin, Italian and English. The evening service on Holy Thursday is more correctly known as the Mass of the Lord's Supper, a significant element of which is the Washing of Feet. In this instance, the Patriarch washed the feet of a number of children who were about to receive their first Communion. I was amused to see that a number of the kids were 'dressing down' for the occasion – jeans and trainers under robes were common. The service concluded with the consecrated Host being taken to a side chapel in readiness for Good Friday Mass.

It was a powerful, solemn experience. The golden glow of the interior of the Basilica, the clouds of incense, the music from the (invisible) choir, the slow procession of the priests and, everywhere, those extraordinary mosaic images from the Bible. It's religion with a capital 'R'.

We returned the following night for the Veneration of Relics. This doesn't have any liturgical significance as a service and didn't attract the same number of people. It was a memorable evening, nonetheless.

The relics were brought out in solemn procession and placed along the iconostasis: a fragment of the Cross, a scrap of Christ's robe, a piece of the column from the Flagellation, two spines from the Crown of Thorns, one of the nails and part of the reed from which Christ, on the Cross, was offered vinegar. Finally, a small crystal vial set in an ornate golden reliquary was set upon the altar. It is said to contain blood from the spear wound. Readings were interspersed with music (beautifully sung antiphonal pieces from Palestrina, Monteverdi and Mozart); following which the relics were carried through the aisles of the Basilica.

Again, as an experience, it was undeniably powerful. As a piece of pure theatre it was extraordinary, reminding me of nothing so much as the Grail ceremony in Wagner's *Parsifal*. But, I ask myself, how much of the emotional impact was due to its theatricality and music? Did I stand there genuinely believing that I was only feet away from the actual Blood of Christ? That, for me at least, was too much of a leap of faith.

Fifty years ago, in *Venice*, Jan Morris wrote of attending the same service, of the same quasi-mystical experience, and of the mundane realities of everyday life that came crashing in upon leaving the basilica. We emerged into a clear Venetian night with a perfect moon above Piazza San Marco and were assailed within seconds by a street hawker trying to sell us some tat. Some things don't change that much after all.

Wagner
'At last, I am living in Venice.'
- Richard Wagner, August 30th, 1858

Richard Wagner's list of dislikes, irritations and petty grievances was not a short one but he genuinely liked Italy, and Venice in particular. His first visit allowed him time to complete *Tristan und Isolde,* as well as serving as a place of refuge from his political enemies, his creditors and his wife Minna. His last visit ended in an argument with his wife, Cosima this time, who accused him of an affair with a Flower Maiden from *Parsifal.* Wagner, stung by her terrible (ie. true) accusation, flew into a rage of, well, Wagnerian proportions, and worked himself into such a state he keeled over from a fatal heart attack.

His rooms, at Ca'Vendramin on the Grand Canal, are available to visit although, as the palazzo is now home to the city's casino, security is tight. You must book in advance, they are strict about numbers, you need to bring along some form of ID and you will probably be met at the entrance by Men with Guns. Entering the country itself seems easier and less intimidating.

Nevertheless, if you are any sort of Wagnerite, this is a place you need to see. It's enormously interesting (there's a fine collection of memorabilia, including letters and scores) and helps to humanise the old monster. He might have been as cuddly as a cactus, but seeing the bills for sending his gondolier out to buy champagne made me think he couldn't have been all bad. One day I hope to be able to stick my head out of our window, hail a passing gondolier and send him off to the shops for champagne. At the moment we'd be sending him off to *Billa* for the 69c 'Clever' wine, but one step at a time.

Venice is not a cheap city but look around and there are a healthy number of free events. One of these was a discussion on Wagner and philosophy, hosted by the Wagner Society of Venice. The weather had been grey and wet all day, which seemed to have hit the audience numbers – just over twenty of us in a space that could easily have held a hundred. Still, it was an interesting evening, and a ninety minute lecture on Wagner and Schopenhauer was a useful workout for our Italian; if not of much practical use on a daily basis.

Home then, the streets still beautiful in the grey half-light. Dinner was a risotto of green vegetables, the lightest of dishes for a spring night. Even if the weather had refused to play ball.

The following morning we ran into the woman who had arranged our flat rental. I got a strange reaction from her when, proudly demonstrating my mastery of the Italian language, I told her the previous night I'd been to a brothel where I listened to an interesting lecture on Richard Wagner.

The misunderstanding, of course, was down to nothing more than a misplaced accent:

Casinò - with the stress on the last syllable - is the place with roulette wheels and card tables.
Casino - with the stress on the second syllable - is a brothel.

A subtle but important difference. She must think British opera lovers are an odd bunch.

La Settimana della Cultura

The weather went into a decline after Easter and it felt like it had been raining solidly for nearly a fortnight. Then Italian Cultural Week (or the *Settimana Culturale*) began, with all sorts of events in town and free entry to state museums.

I'm very fond of the Accademia galleries. They don't get the ridiculous number of visitors that make a visit to the Uffizi akin to a contact sport. Go early enough and you can almost have the place to yourself. A combination of free admittance, a rainy day and at least one school party of bored teenagers made it harder work than it needed to be, however. We took in the first four rooms and decided that was enough.

Back to San Marco then, and the church of San Salvador, for a performance of Brahms's German Requiem by the *Deutscher Aerztechor* – a group of up to 300 German medical professionals who come together a couple of times a year for a series of concerts. In this case, it was a fund-raiser for further renovations to San Salvador. A very laudable aim, although it made me wonder if this wasn't the best weekend to find oneself in Germany with need of a doctor. This was a good performance of one of my very favourite works and, if they seemed a little tired at times, they had done the exact same concert at St Mark's only a few hours previously.

Dinner was another Venetian rabbit from a nice butcher we'd found in San Marco. A splendid, if tiring weekend (we also went to a lecture on Shakespeare at the Teatro Goldoni on the Friday night and, on Saturday morning, a guided tour of the *Pala d'Argento* in San Salvador) which, with the exception of a modest contribution to the church, had all been free.

Lazzaretto Nuovo

On a clear day, you can see the Alps from *Fondamente Nuove*. We'd never managed to see them before until, on our way to catch a boat, we emerged from a *calle* and there they were. Proper mountains, not just specks in the distance, but clearly visible snow-capped peaks against a clear blue sky. A genuine *wow* moment, as if the Almighty had suddenly had a flash of inspiration as to how he could make the most beautiful city in the world even lovelier.

We were in this part of town to catch a boat to the quarantine island of Lazzaretto Nuovo that operated as a decontamination station for ships arriving from areas suspected of being a source of plague. Here the crew would stay for forty (*quaranta* – hence the English word *quarantine)* days, at which point – all being well – they were allowed to proceed on to the city itself.

It served as a gunpowder store during the time of the Napoleonic and Austrian regimes and continued to be used by the Italian army until the 1970s. The island is now deserted, its only guardians being colonies of birds and some suspiciously well-fed looking cats.

It's maintained by volunteers, who arrived on the same boat as ourselves. If you arrived unannounced (it's a request-only stop on the *vaporetto*) the chances are you'd find yourself unable to proceed any further than the locked gate on the jetty, with nothing to do except wait for the next boat passing in the opposite direction.

In the space of four months we had gone from working in a bank to strolling around a disused plague island. It seemed like progress. We passed a faded sign for the Ekos Club of Venice, the organisation that helps to run the place. I misread it as Eros Club and worried that we might be overdressed.

The guided tour was well worth it. The walls are painted with records of arriving ships, together with graffiti-style images of soldiers and boats. The buildings themselves have been remarkably well restored considering the effort it must have taken (our guide described the island, pre-restoration, as 'a jungle').

Entrance, during Cultural Week, should have been free, but we were politely asked if we could make a small donation to the upkeep of the island, which seemed only fair. I took out my wallet, only to find that I had no small denominations at all. But the guy had been so nice, the tour had lasted an hour and they depend on voluntary donations; and so a free visit ended up costing twice as much as the normal charge.

This would normally have thrown me into a right old sulk, but the journey back on the boat snapped me out of it. The view was worth the entrance fee on its own.

La Settimana della Cultura was an exhausting one. A visit to the cloisters and refectory of San Salvador (now part of the Telecom Italia building). A talk on great figures in recent Venetian history at the *Ateneo* and one on Venetian serial killers at the *Casinò*. A number of visits to the Accademia and a hefty number of tours of historic sites. It was like the Edinburgh Festival with less rain.

Guided tours in Italy are not the same as the UK. You must not expect a 45 minute stroll around prior to a cup of tea and a piece of cake in the café. No, these are proper work-outs for the grey matter and there are few minutiae that will not be explored in detail. We attended a tour of the church of San Simeon Piccolo. After an hour we had progressed from the base of the steps to the main door, without, however, any sign of actually going in. At this point we bailed out and went for a drink. And then an ice cream. Then back to the bar as I realised I'd left my bag there (it was still on the back of the chair – note to self, do not try this in Naples or Rome). Then back to the Scalzi bridge to find the crowd still outside the front door. They may very well be there still, no doubt thinking *let's just give it five minutes more, eh?*

An architectural tour of the buildings in the vicinity of San Bartolomeo was spoiled by an annoying bloke who kept constantly interrupting the guide with unrelated questions. After 45 minutes we'd only gone 100 yards and it was becoming hard work, so we knocked this one on the head as well.

In the afternoon, we toured the Palazzo Grimani, only to find Annoying Bloke there again. At least this time he kept his powder dry for the first hour. There was no stopping him once he'd started, however, and progress around the last few rooms slowed to a glacial pace. A number of people looked pissed off, but nobody wanted to say anything, and – being foreign – we weren't really the best people to speak up either. Still, it's a fine building and we were pleased that we were able to understand the majority of an informative talk.

Buoyed up by this, we stopped for a spritz and then dropped by *Ratti* to buy a printer. At which point it became obvious that all we'd learned about the Grimanis and Salviati, of Sansovino and Palladio, was of no practical use at all in an electrical shop in the absence of knowing the Italian for 'toner cartridge'. Or 'USB cable'. Or, indeed, 'printer'. Oh well, Italian lessons would begin shortly.

Aqua (moderately) Alta

Despite numerous visits over the years we'd never been in Venice at a time of high water (it can happen in summer, but it's most likely in autumn or spring) and then, one Saturday night, we heard some sirens go off just as I was cooking dinner. Now, for the new resident, the sound of the *acqua alta* alarm is a bit like the sound of the four-minute warning – namely, you have no idea what it actually sounds like.

Caroline found the official website, where a sliding scale of alarms are detailed from 'you might want to take your wellies out with you' to 'head for high ground immediately'. This was the lowest scale, but nevertheless the man downstairs went out and lowered the *paratia* into place. We had noticed that most Venetian houses had two brackets mounted outside the main door, into which a solid metal barrier could be dropped, with the intention of minimising the amount of water that floods into your property. We had no idea how effective these were.

In the months to come we would find ourselves in the wrong part of town at the wrong time, wading through all sorts of unpleasantness and hoping that the water would not reach top-of-welly level. Nevertheless, from the comfort of a second floor flat, that first sound of the alarm was just a little bit exciting.

Nothing actually happened, which felt slightly anti-climactic. There were a few inches of water in Piazza San Marco on Sunday morning, but that seemed to be it. We were now signed up for warnings by SMS, but it seemed prudent to go and buy some boots as well.

Sunday morning involved a tour round the church of *La Pietà*, the church of the *Ospedale della Pietà*, the orphanage where Vivaldi taught and composed. Even in its day, this was more concert hall than church and nowadays it's difficult to have a look around without buying a ticket for a concert (which will, almost certainly, involve *The Four Seasons*). The Red Priest was dead long before the building was completed, but it seems he may have had some influence on the design: the acoustics, even for the spoken voice, are remarkable, and the sound of the choir and musicians of the orphanage - hidden from view behind screens in upstairs galleries - must have been wonderful. And beyond its musical significance, the church also boasts a number of frescoed ceilings by Tiepolo.

It seemed like destiny, by now, that Annoying Bloke was in our party again. After just five minutes our guide asked if anyone had any questions and our hearts sank as the possibility of lunch seemed to recede into the far distance. Time, however, was on our side as we only had an hour before the next group arrived, so try as he might (and he most certainly did) he was never quite able to get into his stride.

The rain kept us in the flat that afternoon; giving Caroline time to revise her Italian, as I prepared a calf's tongue with olives for dinner. Nicer than you might imagine.

Back to School

Day one of Italian lessons and Caroline had spent the entire night, and much of the previous day, convincing herself that she spoke no Italian at all. I needed to judge the atmosphere with absolute precision here. Should I go straight into full-on Supportive Hubby mode, bouncing along with smiles, hugs and 'it'll be alright's; or was this a situation best played as if nothing untoward was happening at all? I decided this was not the morning to be Mr Life and Soul and chose the latter. It turned out to be the right choice and I awarded myself a bonus Hubby Point.

As it turned out, enrolling was a painless and non-scary exercise. We'd already completed the online application; but there was also a short written test and a brief interview to go through first, in order for them to be reasonably sure of our level. They claimed we were level B2 (or upper intermediate). I thought that was flattering us, but was happy to be flattered anyway.

Our Italian wasn't all that bad. Unfortunately, it wasn't that great either and, given that we first started learning twenty years ago, it really should have been better than it was. I'd wasted my opportunity of working in Italy (it was an English-speaking office and most of my friends were expats); and successive attempts had got stuck in the pattern of starting evening classes with good intentions, and dropping out after a few weeks.

The Great Printer Humiliation excepted, we could just about do everything we needed to; but not with any ease or spontaneity. If The Project was to succeed, we needed to improve. So we signed up for a three-month intensive course with the *Istituto Venezia*, based in Campo Santa Margherita in Dorsoduro; a pleasant twenty minute stroll for us. Four hours a day, five days a week and everything in Italian - five years worth of evening classes condensed into twelve weeks. This, surely, would set us right.

We were a cosmopolitan bunch in our class. Not everybody was there for the long haul, but, at the start, there were three Swiss, two Russians, a Catalan, a Venezuelan, a Colombian, a Japanese woman, a Dutchwoman, an Englishwoman and a Scot. I was the only man, which turned out to be useful as opportunities for gender-related conversation would otherwise have been limited. This set a pattern for the following three months, where male students were consistently outnumbered by women. I have no idea why this should be.

A welcome party had been organised for us at the end of the first day's lessons and I talked to the Dutch lady for a while. It turned out her husband worked for a company called Unisys, at which point I almost choked on my drink. Unisys were the suppliers of a financial payments system, the support of which had utterly blighted my last three years with the bank. I'm sure he's a very nice man and had nothing to do with it, so I told her nothing of the sleepless nights and days of utter horror it had caused me.

The Good Samaritan

There are any number of books, blogs and articles that make Italian bureaucracy sound akin to one of the Circles of Hell that Dante never got around to writing up. If you're like us, you may well have thought that these experiences were overwritten, playing on the worst of Italian stereotypes for comic effect. Or maybe you thought the party involved didn't have a good enough grasp of Italian, or simply hadn't done their research properly. Then, one day, you'll run into a bureaucratic brick wall that seemingly has no way over, under or round it. And then, like us, you'll regret ever having been such a smartarse.

We arrived at the confusingly-titled *ex-Ospedale Giustinian* (confusingly titled because it still *is* an *ospedale*) to register with the Italian Health Service. We had our passports, our *codici fiscale*, our rental contract and bank account statements. Most importantly, we had our S1 forms, which stated that, in the event of us needing health care in Italy, the cost would be picked up by the UK NHS for a period of two years, or until such time as we entered the Italian Social Security System.

The receptionist gave us directions to where we needed to go and the sign on the door did indeed seem to indicate that, amongst other things, this was where foreigners should go to register. There was a short queue, so we took a ticket and sat down to wait.

It took just ten minutes until our number was called and in we went. We'd scarcely begun to explain ourselves when the woman behind the *sportello* shook her head, grabbed a piece of paper with a phone number and address in Mestre, and told us to go away and try there. We attempted to explain that we'd come with our form S1 which needed to be registered here and that it certified our health care would be covered by the UK. She didn't even raise her head to look at it, but shrugged and said she'd never heard of such a form.

We found ourselves back on the wrong side of the door after, at most, thirty seconds. This was soul-destroying. This wasn't a question of language any more, this was just sheer bloody-mindedness coupled with an unhealthy dose of not giving a toss. Neither of us had any faith that the office in Mestre would do anything other than send us straight back here. We really didn't know what the hell to do.

And then something wonderful happened. The man who'd been sitting next to us asked, in English, how we got on. He looked genuinely concerned as we explained. His number was called so he asked us to wait while he had his appointment. Two minutes later he emerged, shaking his head. The *signora,* he apologised, seemed to have no interest in helping people at all. He took out his *cellulare,* dialled the Mestre office and explained the situation. He checked that they recognised the S1 and passed on all our details. He told us what we needed to take, made us an appointment for 8:30 on Monday morning and gave us a contact name there.

We could have hugged him. We stammered a few words of thanks, but he just smiled and said he was glad to help. As we left, he stopped at the main desk and politely, but firmly, remonstrated with the receptionist for not being sufficiently helpful to hapless *stranieri.*

The world may be run by tedious pen-pushers but, just when you need one, there are still a few Lovely Blokes out there willing to lend a hand. Whoever and wherever you are, good sir, we salute you.

To Mestre, then, on the advice of the Saint of Ca'Giustinian. It should just have been a case of registering something that we were entitled to under European law, but it felt more like going into an exam or job interview. Because we weren't 100% convinced that this would work and that we wouldn't be sent off somewhere else; and the long term success of The Project really couldn't be based on us never getting ill or needing any drugs again. Ever.

Happily - mercifully - nothing went wrong this time. A nice lady took us through everything, registered us in the system, assigned us a doctor and that was it. She even reminded us that we needed to update the address on our *codici fiscali* and confirmed that the documentation we now had was suitable proof of health cover when applying for residency. By ten o'clock we were on the train back to Venice and I started a mental list of Nice Ladies as a companion to the list of Lovely Blokes.

That evening I went for an audition with a local choir, *Cantori Veneziani*. I knew they were short of male voices so I should have been in with a good chance but still, this wasn't like buying fish from the market or a newspaper off a stand, this involved making proper conversation in Italian and I really wasn't sure if I'd be up to it. But everyone seemed very kind and cheery, there was a good atmosphere and I sat there thinking *here I am singing with a choir in **Venice** and how on earth has my life turned out like this?* Ninety minutes later I left with a couple of scores under my arm. It had started to rain, but I didn't care. I practically skipped over the Accademia Bridge, the happiest man in Venice.

Bureaucracy

When you join the queue for the *sportello* at the Agency of Entreaties, or the Office of the Anagraphs there are two things you should make sure to do: (1) take a book, (2) take a book. Really.

We waited just half an hour at the *Agenzia delle Entrate*, but that was still a little frustrating as we were only there to tell them we'd changed address. One of the blokes in the queue was obviously an old hand at this game, as he'd worked out that he could stand outside having a ciggie in the sunshine and still keep half an eye on the next ticket being called via the laser display board. Maybe next time we'll bring a picnic and do the same.

Still, they're a helpful bunch at the Agency and once we'd been called it was straightforward enough to sort out. Then it was on to the more forbidding *Ufficio Anagrafe*. If you tell a Venetian that you have an appointment there, they will respond with a dry laugh, a sad shake of the head, a sharp intake of breath, or a combination of all three. Whereas the *Entreaties* are based around the elegant cloisters of the ex-convent of Santo Stefano, the atmosphere inside the *Anagraphs* - despite being based in a *palazzo* on the Grand Canal - is akin to the sort of grim Soviet police station that you might be summoned to after having been Denounced.

Our number was called. It was the woman who had dealt with us last time, fortunately minus her scary colleague. Even more fortunately, we had a post-it note with a list of all the requirements, in her handwriting. She seemed to be on our side this time, although baffled as to how we qualified for Italian healthcare. Oh yes, we had the certificates now, but she didn't understand how we'd managed to get hold of them. She rang another office to check up. Nobody was there of course, so we left with a promise that she'd call us the next day. Slight progress then, but progress nonetheless.

We were prepared for this to take a good couple of days or, possibly, forever; but I got a call midway through Friday morning Italian class. I rushed outside to take it and was informed that yes, all our documentation did seem to be in order and we should come along next Thursday to sign the appropriate forms. I got a round of applause when I reported this back to my classmates.

There was, inevitably, just one more thing. They wanted two letters from the Institute confirming that we really were studying there. I asked the secretary if she could provide them and said it was a request from the *Anagrafe*. She laughed, dryly, with a sad shake of the head and a sharp intake of breath.

We returned to our regular *sportello* the following week. Our *signora* had all the documentation to hand and, after some more form filling, that actually seemed to be it. Her stroppy colleague had returned and occasionally interjected, striking fear into our hearts as she sent our lady off to check with a Higher Authority. Still, less than an hour later, our application for residency was formally in progress and, theoretically, it was now just a matter of verifying that we lived where we said we did for it to be approved.

Let me expand on that. They send someone round to the house in which you claim to be living and so you have to give them a set of times when you will be there. This meant that I would need to stay at home, within earshot of the doorbell, for up to two weeks. At some point someone from the *Comune* would come a-knocking and...well, I didn't really know what would happen after that. I assumed I just needed to show them my passport. I wasn't sure if it would help to have drinks and snacks prepared.

Ruskin
We emerged from the Scuola Grande di San Rocco into the twilight, stiff of back and sore of bottom, after a two-and-a-half hour presentation of a new book on John Ruskin and his time in Venice. We were amongst the hardy bunch who had survived the whole series of lectures, an initially healthy audience having dwindled to a handful over the course of the evening. It had been informative, enjoyable and - like Ruskin's *The Stones of Venice* itself - there'd also been a little too much of it.

Ruskin's attention to detail is staggering, obsessive even. There is scarcely a column, cornice or capital in St Mark's Basilica or the Ducal Palace that is not dissected and analysed in forensic detail. His reasons for this were simple - Venice, he thought, would either fall into ruin or, worse, be destroyed by restoration, and it was important to record what was there as best he could. Admirable, yes, heroic even; but it does not make the *Stones* an easy book to read in its entirety.

He hated half the buildings in the city as much as he loved the other half. He considered the Gothic and the Byzantine to be the high points of architecture, but despised the Baroque (the 'Grotesque Renaissance', as he calls it); whilst Palladio's Classicism drove him into a furious rage ('...*contemptible under every point of rational regard!*').

Nevertheless, he needs to be read. It may not be necessary to read the whole thing (indeed, without being as intelligent as the man himself, it may not even be *possible* to read the whole thing) but he's certainly worth dipping into. When he dismisses a favourite building of yours with his curt (and frequently used) one-liner - '*of no interest*' - you'll want to shout at him, '*oh for God's sake man, just look at the bloody thing, what do you mean it's "of no interest"*'! But he's always erudite and informative, and, more surprisingly, he can also be waspishly funny and magnificently rude.

At the end of his days, he seems to have felt ambivalent about his relationship with Venice, fearing that he had devoted too much of his time and energy to a city that he considered to be dead or dying; more of a museum than an actual functioning city. People are still debating that, over one hundred years after his death. Proof, perhaps, that the old place has some life in it yet.

Earthquake

It was just past four in the morning. We'd had a disturbed night's sleep as an annoying little sod with a loud boat and louder music had passed by twice, but we'd finally drifted off and then...

BANG.

Not loud enough to scare us straight upright out of bed, but nevertheless we were instantly awake and from somewhere came one hell of a banging and a crashing that shook the whole room.

My first thought, in my befuddled state, was that something was wrong with the washing machine, but that wouldn't make the whole building shake. And Caroline doesn't get out of bed to put the washing machine on at 4:00. Then I thought it must be one of the bigger cruise ships passing, but even they don't cause vibrations like this.

Caroline thought it was someone trying to break in. I really didn't want this to be true because he would have had to have been one hell of a big bloke to make the place shake like this and I wouldn't know what to do, other than slide money under the door in the hope he'd go away.

Then the thought hit me - *I suppose it could be an earthquake*. The banging and crashing had stopped, but the ceiling lights were swinging from side to side and the building was still vibrating. Not frightening, but an unpleasant, uncomfortable feeling nevertheless. I went to the window to take a look outside. Whenever an earthquake gets reported over here (and it's not that uncommon), the words *gente in strada* ('people in the street') are used to indicate how serious it is. There was no-one there and no sign of any disturbance at all. I heard the door slam downstairs. Presumably our neighbour was also checking if we needed to get out.

The vibrations died away. I went back to bed, but was unable to sleep. An hour later the aftershock hit - less noticeable this time, just a gentle vibration and, again, the ceiling lights swayed. Caroline didn't wake up at all and so it has now been scientifically proven that my wife is capable of sleeping through an earthquake.

The next day we found out that a quake of about 6 on the

Richter scale had hit just north of Bologna. The shock was felt as far away as Milan. Sadly, people had died. We tend to think that earthquakes just happen in far-off places: easy to forget that they're more common in Italy than any other European country.

The same thing happened two weeks later, this time in class. The room started shaking at about 9:10. Just a little but, as before, an unsettling feeling. Alberto, our teacher, looked up at the light fittings swinging from the ceiling and shrugged insouciantly. 'Ah, *terremoto'*. Some of the students seemed perturbed but he joked that we should perhaps abandon the building and go for a coffee. We all laughed and settled down for the lesson.

We felt the aftershock four hours later. Just a gentle vibration through the building, but noticeable. A German lady in the class was visibly upset and got to her feet. She explained that she was in Rome when the 2009 quake nearly wiped L'Aquila from the map. She really didn't want to sit down, there were only five minutes of the lesson left and so we called it a day.

There was no significant damage in Venice. A statue toppled over in the Papadopoli Gardens and slightly injured a passer-by, but that was about the extent of it. But, of course, we were all thinking the same thing - *if we can feel it here, what's happening a hundred miles away?* You know, of course: over a dozen dead and thousands more made homeless. And it doesn't matter if you're insured to the nines, or that this is a prosperous Western country - the people of L'Aquila are still waiting to be properly rehoused over four years later.

Trousers

One of the strange things about living here is the realisation that hundreds, if not thousands, of strangers throughout the world will have a photograph with you in the background.

We were just about to head off to the *Teatro Malibran*, when I realised I'd put a pair of jeans in the washing machine with a piece of paper in the back pocket that had disintegrated into a million tiny fragments.

So I did what I do when I'm cleaning the rugs - I took them out onto the balcony, checked for passing gondolas and gave them a bloody good shake over the side.

Whilst doing this I noticed a man taking a photograph from a nearby bridge. I assumed he was interested in the view and not myself or, indeed, my trousers, but it's a strange feeling to know you'll be turning up in somebody's holiday snaps. Maybe at a dinner party in a couple of months' time, somebody would look at it, nod sagely and drawl 'ah yes...the beating of clothes above the canal...the Italian peasant still maintains it's the only way to get one's trousers properly clean'.

Home Visit

We had suggested to the *Anagrafe* that the *Comune* could send someone round to verify our address during the afternoons of Monday, Wednesday or Friday.

They came round on Thursday morning.

A note had been left under the door asking me to telephone a Signor Blanco, as soon as possible, between the hours of 8:00 and 9:00. I rang the very next day.

He wasn't there.

Caroline spent Friday afternoon on the *altana*. I spent it skulking and sulking indoors, waiting for the doorbell to ring.

It didn't.

I tried again on Monday. Signor Blanco was a man in a hurry who quickly cut off my garbled explanations in order to tell me that someone would come around at 2:30 that afternoon.

This time he arrived to the very minute. We briefly explained the situation (he chuckled and shook his head when we mentioned the *Anagrafe*), he checked our passports and that was it. He explained that, in the eyes of the Italian State (and possibly the eyes of God) we were not properly married as we hadn't had a Catholic ceremony, but that made no difference to our status as residents. The marriage thing could be sorted out at a later date (there are some minor financial/legal implications) if we got a properly translated certificate.

We shook hands and he headed out into the driving rain. Three days later a letter arrived saying the process was complete...as long as we paid one (final? Oh please let it be final) visit to the *Anagrafe* to sign things off and collect our documentation. Well, I was starting to miss the place anyway. Our *Tessere Sanitarie* had also arrived. We were now officially allowed to be ill and had chipped just that little bit more from the mountain of bureaucracy.

Artichokes

Ascension Day (or the *Festa della Sensa* in the Venetian dialect) celebrates the union of the Most Serene Republic with the sea; symbolised by the Doge throwing a gold ring into the Adriatic. There's a lack of Doges these days, so the mayor gets the job instead. Seemingly every rowing boat in Venice makes its way from San Marco to the Lido, where the ceremony takes place. The mayor arrives on an impressive if slightly kitsch-looking boat recalling the great state barge, the *Bucintoro*, accompanied by the Patriarch. It's a striking spectacle, although if you've seen one regatta you perhaps don't need to see them all.

Our Ascension Day, however, was to be spent at the Sant'Erasmo Festival of Artichokes. I was lukewarm about this. I mean, I like artichokes as much as the next man but they've never struck me as the most festive of vegetables. And something about the very idea of spending Sunday at an artichoke festival made me feel that the rock and roll years were passing me by. Still, Caroline was keen to go and, after having dragged her along to a terrible *Orfeo ed Euridice* at the Malibran, it was her turn to make decisions.

There was already a queue at the stop with thirty minutes to go. Neither of us was keen on the idea of standing in line for half an hour, so I decided there was plenty of time for a spritz. After all, how many people were going to be getting on a boat to Sant'Erasmo on a Sunday afternoon?

Twenty-five minutes later, the answer was revealed as: a lot. Or, to be more precise, One Hell of a Lot. The queue snaked out of the stop onto the Fondamenta and, with a sinking heart, I realised that I was going to be in big trouble if we didn't get on the boat. Somehow, everyone squished themselves on. I assumed that plenty of people would be getting off at Murano, but that turned out not to be the case. If anything, there was a net increase in the number. Things eased slightly at the island of Vignole - it doesn't have much of a population, but if there's only one boat an hour going there it's going to get busy.

We finally reached Sant'Erasmo and enjoyed the luxury of being able to breathe out again. The island serves as Venice's market garden. It's relatively featureless, although the trees and fields (and a handful of cars) are a novelty. It has a small population, but the houses look modern and expensive, and the place has a well-to-do air. The Festival itself, based around the Fort of Maximilian, was a fifteen minute walk along a straight, exposed track that would be unmerciful on a hot summer's day.

We arrived and, well, artichokes! Lots of them! We wandered around to the strains of non-distressing live music, and settled down to a plate of artichokes three ways, along with the roughest 5 euro bottle of red wine either of us could remember. I was forced to admit that this had been a good idea. We took another stroll around and stopped at a stall selling some excellent local wines, where the proprietors were good enough to let us fumble our way through a conversation in Italian. We left for home, many samples later, 20 euros lighter of pocket and, it seemed, members of a Venetian wine club.

We never heard another word from them. But it had been a more interesting afternoon than I might have thought.

Residence

'Patience and Time' - General Kutuzov, *War and Peace.*

We returned to the *Anagrafe* and greeted the Signora with hugs, kisses and flowers. Well, not really, but given that she was, by now, the person we knew best in Venice, it felt as if we ought. She handed over our documentation, pointed us in the direction of the *sportello* that dealt with the issuing of *Carte d'Identita*, and we made our farewells. Ten minutes later, we were standing outside with two spanking new identity cards certifying that we were now Venetian residents, our photos stamped with two metal seals bearing the imprint of The Most Serene Republic. We were now entitled to most of the rights of the Italian citizen, except the right to vote in parliamentary elections. We are however entitled to vote in local and European elections and I am still looking forward immensely to not voting for Silvio Berlusconi.

We had earned a drink. And not just any drink, but a *negroni*. I don't know if you're familiar with the *negroni*? They're a bit like being punched in the face, but in a good way. We stopped at a nearby bar to toast our good fortune. Three months work, disheartening at times to be sure, but everything was now complete. We had health cover, we had a tax code, we had official residency.

I ask the *signora* at the bar if I could pay. She brought the bill and said she remembered us from a few weeks back, when - on account of my wearing a pin-striped jacket – she had mistaken me for a German. Caroline told her why we were so excited.

The *signora* looked taken aback. *Show me*, she asked.

Caroline handed over her *Carta d'Identita*.

She smiled, crumpled the bill in her hands, and knocked a not inconsiderable number of euros off the total. Next time, she explained, we should tell the owner that we were *residenti* and we would not have to pay the same as tourists (*).

There were many reasons for becoming residents: for a sense of belonging, of making a commitment to a new place, of being strictly legal and above board and even the entitlement to free entry to museums. Cheaper *negronis* were an unexpected, but very welcome, bonus.

Patience and Time, indeed.

* We never saw the same waitress again. Neither did we get any more discounted drinks.

Part 4

Residenti

Everything had now changed. We could at last say that we genuinely lived here. We had a place to stay, we had all the necessary paperwork. There would be no more difficult visits to the *Anagrafe*.

I had originally thought that we should start to look for work as soon as we arrived; but Caroline insisted we should take at least six months off. I wasn't at all convinced by this. We needed, I thought, to start earning money as soon as possible; and if it *wasn't* possible, we needed to start thinking about the alternatives.

Of course, she was completely right. The whole process of relocation had been physically and emotionally exhausting; and the intensive Italian classes weren't leaving us much time to relax. It would have been absurdly difficult to job-hunt at the same time and actually attempting to hold down a job would have been impossible.

My concern was that we should at least be sending our CVs out to prospective employers. Caroline pointed out that nobody would be interested in hearing from us in June; and sending out applications into the void, without getting any response, was just going to work me into A State. And, of course, she was right again. If there was work to be found, it would still be there in September. And if there wasn't, well, there was no point in making ourselves miserable before time; and we'd be better able to deal with it if we'd been able to relax and recharge for a few months.

We still had a month of Italian classes left, but after that the summer would stretch ahead of us with no distractions. We would spend it on the *altana*, go to the beach, wander around town and make the most of every last *sagra* or *festa* that came along. Ironically, having just become residents, we found ourselves looking forward to being tourists again.

Three Months

Three months had passed since a water taxi set us down in Campo San Barnaba without so much as a set of keys between us. So were we where we wanted to be?

Geographically: There were days when the bureaucracy seemed impassible and those when we thought we would never get a grip on the language. Strangely enough, there were days when we thought it would never stop raining. And then there were those moments when we took a *vaporetto* home at night, where the only thing to be seen on the Grand Canal was the silhouette of a lone gondolier, and we would think...bloody hell...this is where we *live!*

Financially: I've got to put my hands up here. I thought I'd been pretty brutal on the start-up costs, but I miscalculated. I naively thought we'd be settled into a flat within two weeks. That sort of timescale doesn't seem to be possible in Italy. You can't just see a place you like, give your references and deposit and move in the next day. There are a lot more hoops to jump through. I'd also made no allowance for those banal everyday items that you find yourself needing to buy: a replacement camera (and I'm not pointing fingers here but it was **NOT MY FAULT**), a bedside light, kitchen scales, a mop, beach towels, a fish slice, a dressing gown (we rented a flat with lots of windows in a built-up area, let's say no more eh?). All seemingly silly, insignificant things, but they mount up. We got away with this due to some unexpected cash from our previous employer but still...if you try this yourself be ultra-realistic on the initial costs.

Philosophically: There were times when it was easier for me than for Caroline. The reason for this is simple - I spent most of the 1990s working abroad and so I was prepared for the culture shock (and it doesn't matter how well you know somewhere, when you move there long term there *will* be a culture shock). This isn't meant to sound smug: she spent the decade having a good time in London and Edinburgh. I spent most of it drinking alone in bars in the bleaker industrial towns of the *Ruhrgebiet* and wondering why I didn't have a girlfriend. And yet - if things seemed difficult at times - there were also those moments of chance encounters with lovely Italian people, the pleasures of a free classical concert, of time spent cooking a nice piece of fish for tea, of discovering a fantastically bonkers piece of contemporary opera, of *negronis* that tasted like a friendly punch, of long afternoons in the sun and of those wonderful moments when we would have a proper conversation with someone and think that we really were starting to get a handle on the language. And, ultimately, the realisation that we'd reached middle-age and had never expected to have an adventure again; yet here we were, right in the middle of one.

Yeah. We were where we wanted to be.

Vicini

Pottering about in the kitchen one day, I saw a guy laboriously moving a drumkit out of his front door and strapping it on to a trolley. My first thought was 'Wow. Must be tough moving a drumkit around in this city.' My second thought was 'Hurray! Our neighbour plays the drums!' Or something like that.

So, what are our neighbours like? Truth be told, we still don't really know them. We occasionally saw the people downstairs, but they were often away for long periods and the flat is now lying empty. The place next door is occupied by a French couple who speak no Italian and put their rubbish out at the wrong time. I've swapped *Buongiornos* with one of the guys in the street who evidently isn't allowed to smoke indoors and has to pop outside for a ciggie break. But, on the whole, people keep themselves to themselves. They include :

Artist Woman: occasionally seen at the end of the street, working on one of her big canvases. She's quite talented, but also disappears for months at a time.

Declaiming Bloke: strange fellow in a top-floor flat just across the canal. He hasn't been seen (or, mercifully, heard) for some time. He once kept the entire street awake way into the small hours, reciting something, in English, possibly of a religious nature. People wandered into the street to find out where it was coming from, looked up, shook their heads and went back to bed assuming he couldn't keep it up much longer. They were wrong.

The Party Animals: rarely, but occasionally a problem and twice held parties that went on until dawn. The third time one of the neighbours stuck his head out of the window and screamed abuse until they stopped.

Singers/Musicians: we have a high turnover of these - trumpeters, violinists, pianists, singers. Particularly singers. Some of them have been first class. Others have been, shall we say, *'enthusiastic'*. There is something just a little bit brilliant, however, about living somewhere where your neighbours are likely to burst into a bit of opera when the mood takes them and it doesn't matter if they're not always the best in the world.

Action Movie Guy: a strange one. Every night, around 8pm, he puts on a big action movie at maximum volume. Or possibly - given we never hear any actual dialogue - he just puts on a big action movie soundtrack. As a result, I have become more familiar with the collected works of John Williams than I needed to be. This isn't particularly annoying in itself (he's normally finished by 10pm), the trouble is that he sets off...

Screaming Children: people will tell you Venice is a 'cemetery town', inhabited solely by an ageing population. Not round by us, it isn't. Kids still play football in the streets round here (well, they did, but not for long...in a contest between a canal and a ball there was only ever likely to be one winner) and there seem to be any number of small children and babies in nearby flats. I feel for their parents. Just as they've got the kids off to sleep and start to wonder if they might be able to relax with a glass of wine, Action Movie Guy will decide that what he really wants to hear, RIGHT NOW, is 'Indiana Jones and the Temple of

Doom' turned up to 11. With predictable consequences.

OK, it's hardly Naples on a Saturday night. It's nice that normal people with families live here. I even felt well-disposed to the kids playing football...'isn't this great, you don't see this in the UK any more...'. That sort of thing. And if the Party Animals keep the noise down and people can come to an arrangement with Action Movie Guy (becoming Silent Movie Guy, perhaps?) then we will all continue to rub along just fine.

Strangely enough, the one person we've never heard a peep out of is the drummer.

Human Traffic

It doesn't take long for even the casual visitor to Venice to start identifying those entrepreneurs of the street, eager to separate you from your money.

Bag Men. Street vendors selling imitation Louis Vuitton bags. It's illegal, of course. Sometimes the police will have a crackdown and you see them packing up their wares and high-tailing it at speed, but, on the whole, nothing very much gets done about them. They don't hassle you, which is nice, but laying out great rows of their wares leads to the creation of artificial corridors that make navigating narrow bridges and alleys more of a pain than it ought to be.

Crap Merchants. During the hours of daylight they attempt to sell you a rubbery ball with eyes and feet which, when dropped, splats itself into a gelatinous puddle before miraculously reconstituting itself. Over the course of twelve months I have seen precisely two people stopping to buy these; as well as a tired-looking American tourist in a bar, trying - and failing - to replicate the effect for his son. Yet they're everywhere. After dark, the 'splatty' things are replaced with a sort of flashing gyrocopter device which can be fired into the air from a catapult before slowly floating back to earth. The Crap Merchants are a pain in the arse. It doesn't matter if you are an ordinary couple going about your business. You will still get hassled to buy a splatty rubber ball. And yet, strangely, the minute there's a bout of heavy rain, the Crap Merchants transform into Useful Merchants who will try and sell you umbrellas. Now that's not a bad idea, which leads me to wonder why they don't just try and sell you useful stuff all the time?

Men with Roses. You used to see these guys in the UK. Typically if you've stopped for a drink or a bite to eat, a man with a bunch of roses will approach and try and get you to buy one for your partner. He won't take no for an answer, the idea being that sooner or later you will start to feel like the worst husband in the world if you don't. Many people crack. I, however, am made of sterner stuff. At a restaurant, one evening, a Man with a Rose stopped at our table and practically watched us eat. I thought he was going to pull up a chair at one point but, after I'd handed back the tired-looking plant he dropped on my side plate, he gave up and wandered off to the next table.

Buskers. A mixed bag. The chap who plays the lute on the Accademia bridge in the evening is worth a euro of anyone's money. At the other extreme there's The Worst Busker in the World, a dapper elderly gentleman who saws away tunelessly at an ancient violin on the Rio Tera Foscarini. He's recently reappeared after the winter break (we were starting to worry he was gone for good) and seems to have learned a different tune, bringing the number in his repertoire up to two. He's unfailingly polite, though, and in his own strange way he's also worthy of the occasional euro.

Then there are **Those Who Don't Really Do Anything**. For example, the man who dresses up as Charlie Chaplin and hangs around the environs of the Accademia bridge. That's it. He doesn't actually *do* anything apart from dress up as Charlie Chaplin. Oh yes, he's a master of twirling his cane and standing in a vaguely Chaplinesque way, but that seems to be it. Presumably he must be making some money, but I can't help thinking that it's not what you'd really call an *act*.

Most cryptic of all is **The Petition Against Drugs.** If you have been to Venice you have almost certainly encountered them, typically a small group of people who hang around Campiello San Vidal or Campo San Salvador. You're initially asked if you speak English. If you answer yes, they ask you to sign a 'petition against drugs'. Now, most people in this situation will think that a reasonable request and put their name down. At which point, having engaged you in conversation, they ask you for a donation; by which time you feel too embarrassed to say no and walk on ten euros lighter.

If you stop and think about it, a 'petition against drugs' is so vague as to be meaningless, and how much weight is a petition signed almost exclusively by foreigners supposed to carry? It's the equivalent of those spam emails against drink-driving. If it's a scam, you don't want to part with ten euros; and even if it isn't, you'd be bankrupt within a month if you stopped and signed every time you were asked.

So what is it? Well, contrary to internet rumour, no, they're not going to pick your pockets while you sign. A Venetian acquaintance, whilst vague on the details, tells me that it is a legitimate fund-raiser for a drug rehab charity, even if their method of dragging you in is rather sharp practice. On the last occasion, hard-headed businessman that he is, he suggested to them that surely it would make practical economic and social sense to legalise all drugs. Since then, he has not been hassled further.

It's almost impossible not to get accosted by them. We've tried switching to Italian before the moment of contact. We've tried not speaking at all. We've repeated 'signed, already' in both languages (and, in my case, through the medium of mime that I normally reserve for asking for the bill in restaurants) so many times that one of the girls now gives us a cheery wave and a *Ciao*. And then, one Sunday, we walked straight past them without even an *Excuse Me* or a *Do you speak English*. Never mind the *Codice*

Fiscale, never mind the ID card, never mind the *Tessera Sanitaria*. We felt, at last, as if we truly belonged here. For we had walked unaccosted past the Petition Against Drugs people.

Television

Italy's contribution to world cinema is a great one. In the silent era, before German Expressionism, before the glory days of Soviet filmmaking, the Italians made technical advances that were years ahead of Hollywood. With *Cabiria*, they invented the 'epic' before Cecil B DeMille and DW Griffith. In years to come, Fellini and Antonioni would make classics of European art cinema; and, in the *genre* movie, Mario Bava, Sergio Leone and Dario Argento would redefine and stretch the boundaries of the horror film, the Western and the thriller. It's an extraordinary body of work.

You would not know this from the state of Italian television.

My first encounter with it was during the 1994 World Cup. Amongst the grizzled old pros in the studio was a succession of glamorous female co-presenters, all of whom resembled Anita Ekberg in *La Dolce Vita*. This was a bit of an eye-opener after the UK, where the only concession to glamour was Jimmy Hill occasionally sporting an unusually colourful tie. Nevertheless, even with a shaky grasp on the language, it soon became obvious that their television wasn't that great and, in the intervening years, it had declined further. The blame for this can squarely be laid at the door of Silvio Berlusconi, a man with a seemingly perfect record of taking things that were poor to begin with and contriving to make them worse.

What I'm leading up to is the fact that we haven't got a television. This isn't a grand gesture on our part and I do not think our lives are richer for not having one but, quite simply, what we've seen hasn't convinced us that it's worth the cost of buying one, or the hassle of getting one up the stairs. I would suggest, though, that every critic of the BBC spend one month with nothing to view except Italian television; following which even the most rabid free-marketeer would be begging for the British licence fee to be at least doubled.

Enough of what's bad. What's good? Italian Radio 3 (*Radio Tre*), that's what! You could consider it to be a strange mixture of UK Radio 3 and Radio 4, minus The Archers, but with extra weird things. A mix of news, drama, documentaries, classical music, jazz and general strangeness that I haven't worked out yet. A programme about the film music of Ennio Morricone was suddenly interrupted, for no apparent reason, by a burst of Dire Straits and Pink Floyd. An entire Sunday night was given over to American minimalist composer Terry Reilly (I managed ten minutes of this before Caroline made me turn it off). The weekday opera show appears to be hosted by Statler and Waldorf from *The Muppets*.

Much of the time it's enormously enjoyable and intelligent radio. I love it to bits. I just don't really *understand* it though.

(Don't Fear) The Subjunctive
Or, '*Unusual things about Italian*'.
Or, '*When is a 'Not' not a 'Not'?*'

You can make yourself understood in Italian with a grasp of the *presente*, the *passato prossimo*, the *imperfetto and* the *futuro*; and given that you can express the future using the *presente*, you don't even really need the *futuro*. The trouble is that - if you don't know the other tenses - you'll likely be at a bit of a loss when other people talk to you, or when you're reading a newspaper or book. And if you're going to communicate politely, or with any degree of elegance, you need to engage with the *condizionale* and, above all, with the *congiuntivo* (the subjunctive).

This is a difficult one for English speakers to grasp. We don't often use the subjunctive and, when we do, we don't realise we're using it - think of expressions like 'Be that as it may' or 'If I were you'. But it's widespread in Italian for expressing opinion or doubt, and so this means you need to familiarise yourself with four extra tenses.

Apparently it isn't widely used down south, which made me think that at a point in the future there might be some mileage in *The Naples Project*.

On then, to the *passato remoto*. There is no English equivalent of this. If you went to the pub yesterday, or your great-great-great grandfather went to the pub in 1847, you express it in the same way. Not in Italian. There is an entirely different tense for expressing what happened 'a long time ago'. The most famous example is probably Tosca's aria *Vissi d'Arte* ('I have lived for art') which is perhaps not *quite* grammatically correct - Tosca is, at this point, alive, and not just speaking about the remote past - but certainly sounds more beautiful than *Ho vissuto d'Arte* would have. Again, you might not need to be able to use this in speech, but pick up a novel and you'll encounter it almost immediately.

It turns out, however, that in the south of the country it *is* used in everyday speech. Which immediately put paid to the short-lived *Naples Project*.

This all means that just listening to the radio, or to people talking in the street, is akin to playing bingo. As soon you hear a *'penso che'* or a *'credo che'* you instinctively brace yourself for an oncoming use of the subjunctive. At a lecture one evening by the artist Giuseppe Pennone, I heard a *se* followed by a *congiuntivo* followed by a *condizionale*. I had to restrain myself from punching the air. A textbook example of the *periodo ipotetico*, sir, I salute you!

And then...and then...when you think you're starting to get a handle on all this, you encounter something called the *Pleonastic 'Non'*. Where 'Non' does not mean a negation, but something far more subtle. Think of it as the difference between 'Italian is easier than I thought' and 'Italian is easier than I thought (not that I thought it was going to be hard anyway)'.

Yes, the Italians, bless them, have found a use for the word 'not', that (a) doesn't really mean 'not', (b) doesn't really need to be used, but (c) you still need to be familiar with. And at this point, like me, you put your head in your hands.

Or not.

The Footballer's Fear of the Biscuit

My free Euro 2012 supplement from *Repubblica* contained an article on every European Football Championship and how Italy had performed therein. Some highs (the 1968 victory), some lows (the agonising last minute goal that cost them the 2000 title) and then the darkest moment of all, the 2004 tournament. Cryptically referred to as *Il Biscotto*.

This sent me away to the dictionary where I found, not entirely to my surprise, that a *biscotto* is, actually, just a biscuit. Nothing more.

This confused me - was this a reference to a hitherto unknown performance-enhancing biscuit? - but I thought nothing more of it until the day after Italy drew with Croatia. Not the worst of results and the *Azzurri* were still favourites to go through, but suddenly biscuit fever was everywhere. The sports pages were full of it. Random Italian celebrities were being asked their opinion. Top motorcyclist Valentino Rossi, for example, confidently stated that he had no fear of the biscuit.

What the hell was this all about? It took some research, but I eventually found that it referred to the aftermath of the final game of the first round of the 2004 tournament in which Sweden and Denmark drew 2-2: a result which sent both teams through at the expense of Italy. The two sides, the Italians claimed, had shared the last biscuit between them. It may well have been a coincidence, but the Italians were, and are, convinced that both teams had contrived to fix the result. Shockingly, they claimed, there may have been *cheating*. Ah, Mr Pot, I don't believe you've met Mr Kettle?

At this point I felt like setting fire to my pile of Italian notes. Because memorising the entire Italian dictionary will not prepare you for the fact that, in the language of Dante and Petrarch, a biscuit is not just a sodding biscuit but also 'a contrived result in a football match in which a mutually convenient result is played out'.

Italy had a must-win game against Ireland, but even if they beat them 100-0 they would still fail to go through if Spain and Croatia decided to remove a potentially awkward team from the latter stages of the competition by playing out a 2-2 draw.

Nobody really knew if this was likely to happen or not but, in the hours leading up to the game, all of Italy was living in Fear of The Biscuit.

Gender Politics

As we headed towards the summer break, the choir decided to have an end of term party following the last rehearsal. Every section was therefore assigned things to bring along on the last night, namely:

Sopranos: Savoury dishes
Contraltos: Cakes and pastries
Tenors and Basses: Wine

Now, the more observant among you may have noticed that the female sections of the choir had been asked to do some proper cooking, whereas the men were asked to stop by the shops and pick up a bottle on the way to rehearsal.

It didn't go unnoticed and, by an inevitable coincidence, the last rehearsal was the very same night as the Italy-Ireland game that everyone had been getting into a state about.

Hmm, I thought. Trouble ahead here.

Sure enough, I checked my email on Monday afternoon and found that one brave soul had suggested that if we rattled through the rehearsal quicker than usual we could get to the food and wine before the kick off. In fact, what if we sort of cancelled the rehearsal altogether and just met up for a quick bite to eat between 8:00 and 8:30? Or, if somebody brought a television along, we could all watch the match together?

The responses were swift and brutal, ranging from 'Tell you what, why don't *you* get there early enough to set the entire room up on your own and lay everything out well in advance just so we can all throw this lovingly-prepared food down our throats as quickly as possible?' to 'I have spent hours baking and if you think I'm going to spend the evening sitting in silence as the men gaze open-mouthed at a TV screen you have another think coming.' I'm translating as best I can here, but you get the general idea.

In short, the idea didn't really fly.

We rehearsed as normal and then adjourned to the next room for the *conviviale*. The food was, frankly, splendid, although would it have been quite the same if the men hadn't stopped to pick up some wine along the way? I think not.

It was a very jolly evening. Italy beat Ireland, and Spain did the honourable thing against Croatia. The ghosts of the biscuits of 2004 had been laid to rest, at least for this tournament. But I couldn't help thinking that it was just as well we'd broken up before the quarter finals.

Castelfranco

'...many of his works were sent out of Italy, as things truly worthy to bear testimony that if Tuscany had a superabundance of craftsmen in every age, the region beyond, near the mountains, was not always abandoned and forgotten by Heaven.' - Giorgio Vasari, 'The Lives of the Artists: Giorgione of Castelfranco'.

Castelfranco is an historic walled town, 40km from Venice. It's worth a visit in its own right but the main attraction is the cathedral which houses the *Castelfranco Madonna,* one of a handful of undisputed works by Giorgione, the most mysterious artist of the Italian Renaissance.

We know very little about him. Vasari's chapter on him is one of the shortest in the whole of the *Lives.* He had probably been a student of Giovanni Bellini, but opinion is divided as to whether he was Titian's master or if they were just colleagues.

He seems to have been a handsome if foppish-looking fellow, judging by his statue (a recent one but based on what may be a self-portrait) and died a suitably romantic death at an early age. Vasari claims that Giorgione, always something of a ladies' man, went to visit his lover without realising she was carrying the plague; with unfortunate, if predictable, consequences.

There is no firm agreement on the number of works in existence that can be definitively attributed to him. It may be as few as six. Three of these are in Venice: a sad fragment of fresco from the outside of the Fondaco dei Tedeschi, and two works in the Accademia - *La Vecchia* and the mysterious *La Tempesta.* Mysterious in that nobody really knows what it represents - it's not based on religious or classical themes, if it's an allegory it's an impenetrable one, and the one thing we know with certainty is that it isn't really called *La Tempesta.* Giorgione. He's very mysterious.

The *Castelfranco Madonna* was commissioned by the mercenary Tuzio Constanzo in honour of his son Matteo, who had died of a fever during military service.

It's a variation on the standard *sacra conversazione* and the composition is the classic triangle-within-rectangle style, but with a number of intriguing differences. It's assumed the figure on the right is St Francis, but the armoured figure on the left is more difficult to identify – he may be Saint George, local boy St Liberalis, or Matteo Constanzo himself. The coat-of-arms beneath the Virgin's throne is that of the Constanzo family, and the tomb and paved floor reflect the space of the chapel in which the painting is housed.

The background is most likely that of Castelfranco c.1505 and the importance given to the landscape is another thing that marks this work out as unusual - it wasn't that common in Venetian painting of the time and Giorgione's use of it may have influenced his master Bellini. Great as he was, Bellini wouldn't have been able to resist adding in a cloud of *putti* and an extraneous angel or two. Giorgione, however, keeps the composition clean and uncluttered, save for two tiny figures in the background. Because this painting isn't meant to inspire us to great, devotional thoughts - it's inviting us to pay our respects to the young Matteo.

Whatever it 'means', it's a genuinely magnificent work. There were five of us in our group, and we stood and looked at it and discussed it for almost thirty minutes. When you see the *Mona Lisa*, or the *Primavera*, or the *Birth of Venus* you share the experience with hundreds of other people and the incessant click and flash of cameras. But in this quiet chapel, in a town just one hour from Venice, you can stand and look at one of the great paintings of the world and pretty much have it all to yourself.

Art Night

Art, architecture, dance, music, cinema: Venice is not short of festivals. Yet the city still thought it could squeeze another one in, in the shape of *Art Night Venezia*. This is a spin-off from the 'White Night' events that started in Russia and made their way across Europe: mini-festivals that start in the late afternoon and continue through the night.

We began by joining the queue outside Ca'Foscari University for the opening event. Except that after twenty minutes we were none the wiser as to what the opening event actually *was*. We'd assumed there'd be a couple of speeches and a glass of wine or two, but neither of them seemed to be forthcoming. A free bag was as far as it went.

We moved on to the university's architecture department, which promised re-enactments of historic pieces of performance art. We were there to see Yoko Ono's 'Cut Piece' in particular, but things were running late so we began with a work entitled 'Meat Joy' (Carolee Schneemann, 1964. I had to look her up) in which a woman smeared processed meat over her body whilst an accomplice in the audience threw bread rolls at her. I guess it's a metaphor for the body and sexuality but my immediate reactions were (1) this is why people don't really *get* contemporary art and (2) I never want to eat a hamburger again.

'Cut Piece' - in which members of the audience snip away at the clothing worn by the artist – has become an iconic work. It was re-staged by a male lecturer from the university and I suppose one might say that this changes the nature of the piece. Nevertheless, it was, intriguing to watch, if a little unsettling towards the end as a nasty edge entered into it: one participant clipped away a length of cloth and tied it around the artist's neck, whilst another blindfolded him.

It was tempting to stay and watch all the others, but we decided to head off to the Palazzetto Bru Zane. This is a gem of a place, a beautiful 17th century palazzo that now serves as a concert hall and centre for research into French music of the Romantic era. We listened to a string quartet by Hyacinthe Jadin (I'm afraid I had to look him up as well) followed by a guided tour. A lovely place and well worth a visit.

It was time for a quick bite to eat at the *Due Colonne*, where the quality of their pizza needs to be balanced against

Fawltyesque levels of service. I chose unwisely with a topping of shredded, smoked horse; which had a certain novelty value but didn't need to be tried again.

Off to Ca'Pesaro, which serves as Venice's gallery of modern art and which promised a live performance of 16th century lute music to accompany a stroll around the galleries. Unfortunately, this one hadn't been properly thought out, as the other attraction was a demonstration of Martial Arts on the ground floor; and so the lutenists - no doubt feeling unable to compete with the blood-curdling screams from below - had not put in an appearance.

It's an interesting collection but we could come back here at any time and so - given the absence of lute music - we decided to move on. It was unmercifully hot and humid, but the Telecom Cloisters at San Salvador were quiet and cool, and offered the chance to relax with some big-screen video art and a glass of ice-cold prosecco.

We thought about staying for the whole set, or at least until the prosecco ran out, but we went back to the Accademia Bridge for a short, but beautiful, video projection on to the facade of the Palazzo Cavalli-Franchetti. It was past 11:00 by now and - to be honest - going home for a big sleep seemed like the most attractive option. But that would have been cheating, so we headed off to the Palazzo Cini. Thrillingly, they have a Piero della Francesca. Less thrillingly, it was on loan to a museum in Perugia.

We made it to the Peggy Guggenheim collection, with just twenty minutes remaining. And, well, it left us a bit cold. It's impressive, yes, but I found the atmosphere smug and self-congratulatory, and the whole 'Cult of Peggy' thing is tedious.

Home then, and a past-midnight spritz on the balcony. I had never been so hot in my life. Removing my t-shirt was akin to being waterboarded. It had been a splendid evening. I felt enormously grateful, though, for the fact that Art Night comes but once a year.

Luigi Nono

We were waiting for a boat over to Giudecca from the San Basilio stop, taking shelter from the sun in the shade of a nearby bar, when the barman overheard our discussion and chipped in.

'Luigi Nono?', he smiled, 'Ah yes, I knew Luigi Nono!'

We asked if he had any stories.

He shrugged apologetically.

'Well, he was a good man. But I found his music quite difficult.'

'Difficult' is fair enough. Nevertheless, Luigi Nono is probably the greatest post-war Italian composer (and despite that giant Puccini-shaped shadow, a case could be made for him being the greatest of the entire 20th century). During the 1950s he coined the phrase the 'Darmstadt School' to describe the work of himself, Pierre Boulez, Karlheinz Stockhausen and Bruno Maderna in attempting to create a new form of Western music; a form that would be free of the nationalist associations that had been appropriated by the Third Reich. But Nono had little interest in creating purely abstract music - his works are inspired by architecture, literature and poetry, and are fiercely political. He died in 1990, but his archive was established in 1993 under the care of his widow.

The archive isn't far from the Palanca stop, housed in the cloisters of Sant'Eufemia, which also serve as artists' studios. Nuria Schoenberg Nono, Luigi's widow and Arnold Schoenberg's daughter, was there to greet us and show us around the archive. There are stage designs for his operas (or 'stage works' as he preferred to call them) and a complete set of scores; together with his private library, photographs, video and audio recordings. The photographs are a Who's Who of late 20th century music: the Darmstadt years show a handsome young Nono together with a glamorous pipe-smoking Nuria; along with Boulez and an earnest-looking young Stockhausen. Most interesting perhaps are Renzo Piano's designs for *Prometeo*, premiered at the disused church of San Lorenzo and conducted by Claudio Abbado. Because, in a city where one can hear *The Four Seasons* every night of the week, the fact that three artists of the stature of Nono, Piano and Abbado staged such a work in the late 20th century gives lie to the cliché of the 'museum city'.

Nono's work is more popular in Germany than anywhere else these days - he never seems to have quite caught the imagination in Britain - but Nuria was pleased to hear that we had been able to see *Al Gran Sole, Carico d'Amore* at the Edinburgh Festival, some years back.

I chatted with her about Nono's interest in architecture and his friendship with Carlo Scarpa. She asked if we still lived in Edinburgh and I explained how we'd moved to Venice, after leaving our jobs in IT. She smiled. Ah, they are always having trouble with their *informatica* - the machines are old, the network is slow, some of the applications no longer work.

I agreed. It's always the same with IT, isn't it? Something becomes out of date as soon as it's out of the box. But if I could be of any use, I'd be more than happy to help in any way.

She smiled again and thanked me. We had to leave at that point, so I had no idea if she was just being nice, or if I should turn up for work on Monday morning.

I had just passed ten minutes discussing IT strategy with Arnold Schoenberg's daughter. This was simultaneously the coolest and the nerdiest thing that I had ever done in my life.

Verona

We made a short trip to Verona in early July, for a night at the opera in the Roman Arena. It was a toss-up between *Aida* and *Turandot* and - given that the latter was only on in August, when we could expect it to be even hotter - *Aida* won. Anyway, it's surely the quintessential 'stadium opera' and, if we were only going the once, we wanted to have the full experience.

The bus from Verona railway station to our hotel didn't take us through the nicest part of town and by the time we arrived at our hotel - on a busy street thick with traffic fumes – I was starting to regret ever leaving Venice at all. But as we walked into town that evening, I realised that I'd done it a disservice: the town centre, the views across the river Adige and the pink marbled streets are all lovely.

A friend at the *Istituto* had recommended a place to eat, *Al Bersagliere*, which turned out to be one of those rare places where you want to eat absolutely everything on the menu. It's rare for us to feel up to the whole antipasti-primi-secondi experience, but this time we thought we had to give it a go. We split a starter of polenta with *sopressa*, *lardo* and cheese; moved on to a frankly awesome risotto with Amarone; and then Caroline had a veal escalope in a white wine sauce, while I had a fillet of beef that could be cut with a fork. I still had room for a *diplomatico* (a *pan d'oro* with caramel) for dessert as well. In fact, I was on such a roll, I considered saying 'Bring the menu back my good man and let's start again from the beginning eh?'

Time, sadly, was getting on, so I went up to pay the bill. Three courses, a dessert and a bottle of Amarone - in Venice, a meal of this quality would be eye-wateringly expensive, but here we got change from a hundred euros.

I noticed a series of photographs showing the owner in the company of various people. I assumed they were celebrities but I didn't recognise any of them until I suddenly did a double-take...

'Erm, isn't that the Archbishop of Canterbury?', I said.

He beamed, '*Si*! Mr Williams! He is my friend!'

The two of them, it transpired, had been at a function in Rome, organised by the Pope, and the Archbishop had given him his official invite as a souvenir. And there they were, shaking hands, a demob-happy Williams looking cheerier than he had in years. I wondered why we never got invited to those sorts of parties.

I can't recommend this place highly enough and hope that next time we'll see a picture of our genial host with the Dalai Lama.

On then, to the opera. We passed a number of bars along the way, already filling up in readiness for the Italy-Germany semi-final. We took our seats. The production was a re-staging of the classic one from 1913 and the sets looked as traditional as one could wish for. The arena slowly filled, the orchestra took their seats and the opera began.

The strains of the overture faded away. The singers moved forward. Almost silent now. The drama was about to begi...

WWWWWHHHOOOOOOOOOOAAAAAAAAHHHHH!

Italy, presumably, had scored.

This set the tone for the next couple of hours. There was the occasional WHOOOOAAAAHHHH but never quite enough to suggest that they'd scored again. And then there came a sudden cacophony of BEEEEPS from scooters, joining in with the WHOOOAAAAAAHHHHSS and, as I checked my watch, I realised that it was full time. They must have won. The traditional post-match celebration of riding around on *motorini* and BEEEEPing had begun.

The third act wasn't really able to compete.

And the opera itself? Well, seeing a production of this age makes you understand why staged opera had to change. Yes, there was a cast of hundreds and it was often beautiful to look at; but any sense of drama was lost in the spectacle and the acting never really got beyond the old-fashioned 'stand and deliver' style.

The other problem is that the Arena, obviously, doesn't have all the technical advantages of a modern theatre, so scene changes take a long time; with the result that a show that started at 9:15 didn't end until 1:00 in the morning. And in these seats (and these weren't even the cheapest ones), that's a lot of time. Yes, we'd read about the famously uncomfortable seating, but nothing can prepare you for the reality. They are, quite frankly, bum-achingly uncomfortable; and I speak as one whose buttocks endured *Tristan und Isolde* at Bayreuth without complaint.

That apart it was an extremely enjoyable evening and the football actually added to the atmosphere. Would I recommend it? Well, if you're a purist, beware: there will be regular flashing from cameras and - during the big numbers - applause will start before the orchestra has finished playing. But it's not really a place to listen and watch in reverential silence. Here, the shared experience is the important thing. If you have an interest in opera, then, yes, it's a place you need to go to, at least once.

But for God's sake, take a cushion.

Heatwave

By the first week of July I had decided that enough was enough and it was finally too hot to keep wearing a jacket. I didn't do this lightly. I don't *like* not wearing a jacket. Wearing one, I look like a man about town. Without one, I look like a man without a home, and I miss all those useful extra pockets. When I went into school in shirt-sleeves, the rest of the class applauded.

This may give you an idea of how hot it had become.

An anti-cyclone somewhere off North Africa was fanning hot air in the direction of Northern Italy. Everyone said it had been the hottest June in memory. Temperatures were around 30° during the day, but it felt much hotter. It was impossible to keep cool, or even to keep dry. Humidity was at 90% and I wondered if we would actually drown in the event of it hitting 100.

So in the space of little more than two months I had made the journey from hat and coat, to jacket, to shirt-sleeves and (God help me) even the occasional outbreak of shorts and sandals. There was now only one place left to go, namely sitting around the house in my pants, and nobody wanted that to happen.

The Italian meteorological office gave these anti-cyclones wonderful classical names. We sweltered our way through *Scipio, Charon, Ulysses, Minos, Nero* and *Caligula*, only to find that the none-more-ominously entitled *Lucifero* was soon to blow into town. The Met Office were playing a dangerous game here, as there really was nowhere to go after that; and so they ran the risk that an even hotter one could yet arrive and they'd be forced to call it *Keith* or *Nigel*.

There was, I suppose, an irony in having gone to great pains to rent a flat with a balcony only to find it too hot to be able to sit outside. Not a problem we ever encountered in Leith. I was proud of my self-restraint in never using the words 'So....remember that flat I liked that had air-conditioning?'

Malamocco

The district of Malamocco, on the Lido, is one of the very oldest parts of Venice, dating back to the 6th Century when it was established by refugees from Padua.

Sometime during the 12th Century, a fisherman on the lookout for firewood found a suitably hefty log and took it back to his house. The following morning, he found that it wasn't where he'd left it. Off he went and, to his surprise, found it in the exact same place from which he'd taken it the previous day. Strange, but it was evidently a very good log because he dragged it home once more.

The following morning, again, it was nowhere to be found. So he went out and brought it home for a third time, with predictable results. Now, you might think that this was just God's way of saying *go and pick a different log*, but our boy was made of sterner stuff, went back to the same place and, for his pains, was rewarded with a vision of the Virgin. This time he used the log to carve a statue of the Madonna and Child which, to this day, stands in the church of Santa Maria Assunta. And every year, a *sagra* is held to celebrate the event.

Our guide was Riccardo, a resident of the Lido and a lovely, hippyish chap. By day, he teaches Italian to immigrant schoolchildren. By night he plays bass in fearsome-sounding Venetian Heavy Metal band *HausMaster,* although he bemoans the fact that, unlike Germany or the UK, Italy does not really have a 'Metal' culture. He believes that English is 'the language of Metal' and that he learned more from the lyrics of Iron Maiden than he ever did at school. He cheerfully admits that his English would be somewhat limited once conversation progressed beyond the themes of Death, Destruction and the Great Beast.

The *sagra* is small in scale, but there's a good atmosphere to Malamocco. It's little more than a couple of streets, but it has something of the feel of a mini-Venice in the countryside and a genuine sense of community.

We took a look around the church (the priest was delighted to have visitors and showed us round everything, prior to insisting that we take some fruit from the garden) and visited a couple of art exhibitions. Then an archery demonstration caught my eye because, instead of the usual bull's eye target, they were using the image of the Welsh flag. Now, it's possible that the great Wales - Venice conflict was one of the more unusual episodes in European history, and I really should have been paying more attention in school that day; but I suppose it's more likely that they just thought it a striking image to engage the kids. The elderly gentleman in charge asked me if I could write something in the visitors' book, in Welsh. It's been thirty years since I used it in anger, but I can still remember the odd bit, and I thought the chance of a native speaker wandering along and shaking his head at the lamentable standards of Welsh language teaching in Malamocco was pretty remote. I limited myself to writing *Hwyl Fawr* and a translation (*significa 'Buona Fortuna')*. He seemed disappointed at my indecipherable scrawl and added the words *in lingua gallese* next to it, in case anyone should be in any doubt.

A band was setting up for later on and a number of stalls were selling local produce, but we feared a losing battle with the mosquitoes and so made our way back to the *vaporetto*.

There may not be a huge amount to see, but it's still a nice little place and a refreshing change of pace from the hustle and bustle of the main islands. If you're in Venice for a long period, it repays a visit.

School's Out

Three months of intensive study came to an end with a brutal two hours on pronomial verbs and a rather more enjoyable discussion of Dante. I was proud of the fact that I had read the whole of the *Divina Commedia*. Not just the famous bits, not just the gorier parts of the *Inferno*, but the whole flippin' lot, albeit in English. I felt quite smug for approximately 10 seconds, until one of the other students said she had read it in its entirety in *Italian*. This was both deflating and confusing at the same time. If you can read the whole of the *Commedia* in the original language, you should surely be teaching Italian instead of studying it.

I had mixed feelings about finishing. I had enjoyed almost every minute of it, even the pronomials and the pleonastic *non*s. Studying had given a structure to our days, as well as a ready-made social calendar and supply of friends. I also had the nagging thought that one month, just *one* month, more and I would truly, properly master this language.

And yet latterly there had been the occasional moment of thinking that old ground was being covered. Perhaps it was now more important to step back, to take stock of everything we'd covered and get out there and speak Italian.

Caroline enjoyed it somewhat less than I did, because our minds work in different ways. She used to be a systems analyst - in other words she likes to revise and review everything until it's absolutely perfect. I was a programmer - I just get on with things and, if it isn't 100% correct, well, I can usually put it right without

117

too much harm being done. This is a useful attitude for learning a language (it is also a terrible attitude for pursuing a career in IT).

The *Istituto* claimed to have dragged us up to level C1 ('Effective Operational Proficiency') of the Common European Language Framework, which is nearly as good as it gets. Even now, this is flattering us. Still, if there was no danger of us being mistaken for locals, we could now do everything we needed to and it was something to build on. If you want to improve your Italian at the same time as taking a break in Venice, I highly recommend them.

Redentore

'And Darkness and Decay and the Red Death held illimitable dominion over all' - Edgar Allan Poe, 'The Masque of the Red Death'.

Titian's *Pietà* is my favourite painting in the Accademia. Dating from 1575, it's generally regarded as being his final work and the kneeling figure of Nicodemus before the body of Christ is probably a self-portrait. The impression is one of absolute despair, of a flickering source of light being slowly crushed under the weight of the encroaching darkness. There is precious little hope in this painting and with good reason: Venice was in the grip of a plague that would kill a third of the population. Titian, a devout man, painted this as an act of supplication, as a plea for himself and his son Orazio to be spared. It didn't work. The plague took them both, along with nearly 50,000 others. The citizens of Venice believed it to be a punishment from God. It must have seemed like the very end of the world.

The disease burned itself out in its own good time. In July 1576 the city was declared plague-free and, in 1577, ground was broken on Andrea Palladio's church of *Il Redentore* ('The Redeemer'), commissioned in thanks for the city's deliverance. To this day, the city celebrates the *Festa della Redentore* on the third

Sunday in July.

Our *Redentore* started on the Thursday night, with a performance of *La Maschera della Morte Rossa*. Devoid of dialogue and barely a few pages in length, Poe's story is a difficult one to stage. This was a clever adaptation, however, and it worked very well - a narrator related the story, which was acted out with a mixture of dance, music and *commedia dell'arte;* whilst the mirrored hall of the Palazzo Zenobio was the perfect space for it (**warning**: do not sit in the front row of any performance in which the words *commedia dell'arte* are mentioned - your participation will be expected, nay, insisted upon).

On Friday night, we caught a boat to Giudecca and made our way to *Il Redentore* for a concert of early Italian Baroque music. Palladio's church is notable for its cleanness of line and simplicity. There are no great baroque tombs or spiralling columns here. The overall impression is of space and light. Some might think it overly cold and clinical, but it could equally well be considered a perfect response to the circumstances that led to its commissioning. The concert itself - Monteverdi, Frescobaldi, Schuetz *et al* - was first class; excellent playing and singing from the small group of musicians, filling the space wonderfully.

Saturday is the eve of the *Festa*. In the past, a bridge of boats would be constructed across the Giudecca canal. That stopped some years ago and, today, a temporary pontoon is used instead. At 7:00pm, Capuchin monks from the *Redentore* set out across the bridge to greet the Mayor and the Patriarch, who then make their way back to the church to light candles in thanks; shortly followed by what seems like the entire population of Venice.

The festival has a reputation as the most 'local' of Venice's celebrations and foreign accents were drowned out by Italian ones. The Zattere and the Giudecca were lined with people, many of whom were setting out chairs and tables, food and drink, in preparation for a long night. Others just arrived in their boats and dropped anchor in the *bacino* - fewer than usual, however, due to the recent introduction of controversial new licensing measures.

We considered crossing the bridge, but the sheer weight of the crowd put us off and we retired to Nico's for *negronis*. An indulgence, yes, but still, the *Redentore* comes but once a year. Then home for dinner, following which we took a bottle of wine and some deckchairs up to the *altana* to watch the fireworks. I thought we might have been spoilt by years of the Edinburgh fireworks at the Festival and Hogmanay, but there was something incredibly special about seeing the city lit up like this.

Sunday felt clearer and cooler after an almighty storm, which sadly brought down all the lanterns lining the Zattere. There was still a steady stream of traffic on the bridge, but we finally took our stroll over the canal to the church. An odd feeling, despite the fact we'd made the same journey by *vaporetto* any number of times. Masses were being held round the clock at the *Redentore*, with candles being consumed at such a rate that a server was having to use a fish slice to clear away excess wax.

We made our way back across the only-slightly-ominously wobbly bridge. A regatta of small boats was taking place in the canal and, if you screwed your eyes up and tried to ignore Porto Marghera and the floating gin palaces, you could convince yourself that things really hadn't changed that much at all.

Brief Encounters

We were now left to our own devices for the first time since we arrived. There was no more red tape to deal with and we were no longer starting the day with four hours of Italian. Everything seemed that little bit more normal - get up, go to shops, get the paper; and then home for two hours of Italian revision and two hours of job hunting.

We may no longer have had the *Istituto* to organise our social lives for us, but we still managed to entertain ourselves. We went to a concert by the orchestra of *La Fenice*. Now, *La Fenice* is not a cheap place to get into, but this was a one-off 'Opera Gala' in the courtyard of the Ducal Palace, conducted by the great Korean Myung-Whung Chung; featuring an all Verdi/Puccini programme for a relatively modest thirty euros each.

We picked up our tickets and, finding ourselves with some time on our hands, thought we could sneak a swift one in. The area around Piazza San Marco is not the place to find oneself in need of a quiet drink, but nevertheless we found somewhere only a couple of streets away. A strange little place with an interior festooned with girly calendars. I'm not sure what sort of market they were aiming at, but perhaps it wasn't the middle-aged classical music fan.

So we stood outside with our drinks, and I was pondering that, presumably, it was somebody's job to turn all those calendars over on the first of every month, when Caroline dug me in the ribs. I was about to protest that I hadn't even raised my eyes from my prosecco when she pointed to a gentleman of South-East Asian appearance strolling past. *That's him, isn't it? That's the conductor.*

I wasn't convinced, as I'd seen Myung-Whung before and I thought he was somewhat older and greyer. I said he was probably just a tourist, albeit one armed with something that looked like a music folder.

But, thirty minutes later, in the splendid surroundings of the Ducal Palace, it turned out that I was wrong, as the very same gentleman walked to the podium. It had indeed been Mr Chung. My apologies Maestro, you are clearly much younger than I thought.

This brought to mind an incident of a few days previously, when I had almost bumped into the Patriarch of Venice. Literally. I turned my head and there he was, hurrying past in his work clothes. It struck me that the city is a great leveller. The very nature of the place makes it unlikely that you can be chauffeured from post to post and so the great and the good have to get around town in the same way as the rest of us, whether they be a famous international conductor, God's Representative in Venice, or a pair of unemployed ex-IT workers.

It was a splendid concert. With a decent orchestra, singers and conductor you can't go wrong with a programme of best bits from *Butterfly, Tosca, Boheme, Don Carlo, Traviata et al*; and the setting made it that little bit more special. We got an *encore* of the *William Tell* overture (Chung's an enjoyably 'visual' conductor when he has something like this to get his teeth into) and the *Brindisi* from *La Trav*; which sent everyone home in a good mood.

We set off back to Santo Stefano, passing some musicians from the orchestra along the way. Just making their way back home through the *calli* like the rest of us.

Beyond the Four Seasons

Stravinsky in the 20th Century. Wagner in the 19th. Mozart in the 18th. Monteverdi in the 17th. Venice has been a magnet for great composers from the time of the Flemish musicians who came here in the 15th and 16th centuries. Most significant of those, perhaps, was the figure of Adrian Willaert who became the *Maestro di Cappella* at San Marco in 1527. Remaining until his death in 1562, he transformed the city's reputation from a relative musical backwater into one of the greatest in Europe. Composers came from all over the continent to study with him. Amongst his pupils was the great Venetian Andrea Gabrieli - an indelible link between the 'Venetian School' and the music of the Low Countries.

We attended a concert of polyphonic Flemish music at San Moisè one Saturday night. Now, San Moisè is a very, *very* strange church. As soon as you enter, the eye is drawn to the huge altarpiece, by Heinrich Meyring, of Moses receiving the Ten Commandments on Mount Sinai. Or, to be more precise, an almost actual-size reproduction of Mount Sinai. You have to admire the sheer bonkers ambition of it, even if the overall effect raises a smile instead of a sense of awe, which presumably wasn't Meyring's intention.

The programme itself was a selection from some of the greatest composers of that period - Ockhegem, Dufay, des Prez and Willaert himself. This is diabolically difficult music to sing and - with just four singers - there was no way that mistakes could be hidden. But if there was the (very) occasional problem of intonation, it didn't detract from the all-round excellence of the performance. Fantastic music-making and the fact that a concert of this quality was free was extraordinary.

Adrian Willaert is an unsung hero these days. By contrast, you couldn't get away from Vivaldi if you wanted to. You can see a concert of his works at San Vidal or the Pietà almost every night of the week. Now, these are professional musicians, so it's fair enough to expect a certain standard of performance, but the problem is this - if you had to saw your way through the *Four Seasons* night after night after night, you would be forgiven for becoming a little stale. Do yourself a favour and seek out some of the free music in Venice. And save a few euros into the bargain.

Bottarga
Bottarga: dried tuna or grey mullet roe, cured in sea salt. It doesn't sound like the most appetising thing in the world. We'd tried it a few years ago, in Sicily and thought it was nothing more than OK.

Still, one of the fishmongers in Campo Santa Margherita told us that he'd acquired some tuna with their roe and was having a go at making his own. He seemed pleased that we showed an interest in what was going on. So much so that, one Saturday, Caroline arrived back from shopping with a great slab of the stuff that he'd given her for free; and nothing says 'welcome to Venice' quite like free things from the fishmonger.

So despite finding it underwhelming last time, I set to work on finding some recipes. There aren't that many and they don't stretch much further than these :

'Bruschetta with Bottarga'
Ingredients: bread, bottarga
Method: grate bottarga over bread

'Pasta with Bottarga'
Ingredients: pasta, bottarga
Method: grate bottarga over pasta

Spaghetti with bottarga it was, then. There are any number of recipes, but I went with the *River Cafe* book. I don't know why, but I've kind of got it into my head that the *Silver Spoon* is for a regular tea, but *River Cafe* gets pressed into service for something a bit more special.

Except that this recipe seemed a little odd. Admittedly I was scaling down the quantities but that only required the ability to divide by three and I was pretty sure I'd got it right. It seemed to require 175g of spaghetti to 250g of bottarga. Which was the entire chunk. It seemed like a hell of a lot. I cut a small piece off and nibbled away pensively. Quite nice, but it also packed a hefty anchovy-like flavour and a quarter kilo of the stuff was going to make the dish a little *assertive* to say the least. Nevertheless I was prepared to give it a go and got ready to start grating away.

Caroline, sensibly, was less convinced and checked out various recipes on the internet. Strangely enough, there seemed to be no common agreement on quantities beyond the basic one of 'more bottarga than spaghetti is insane.'

In the event, I used a third of it and it was absolutely delicious. Here, then, is the adapted recipe.

'Bottarga Jonesy Style'

Ingredients (for 2): 175g spaghetti. 60g grated Bottarga. As much garlic and parsley as you can be bothered to chop finely. Half a de-seeded dried chilli. (I'd use a whole one. Caroline wouldn't use one at all. We compromised.)

Method: while the spaghetti is cooking, gently fry the garlic in a healthy slug of olive oil. Throw in the parsley and half the bottarga. Throw in the drained spaghetti, give it all a good stir and then sprinkle the rest of the bottarga on top. Eat, with copious quantities of wine. Any colour will do.

A twenty minute tea and, thanks to our friendly fishmonger, practically free. And if you're using *River Cafe*, don't forget to double-check those quantities.

Arsenale

> *....as in the Arsenal of the Venetians*
> *boils in winter the tenacious pitch*
> *to smear their unsound vessels over again*
> *for sail they cannot; and instead thereof*
> *one makes his vessel new, and one recaulks*
> *the ribs of that which many a voyage has made;*
> *One hammers at the prow, one at the stern;*
> *This one makes oars and that one cordage twists;*
> *Another mends the mainsail and the mizzen.*
> - Dante, 'Inferno', Canto XXI, verses 7 - 15

Dante is still remembered at the *Arsenale*, his verse being set into the wall behind a pride of lions sculpted by people who might have heard of them but had only a vague notion as to what they might look like.

Dating back to the thirteenth century, the Arsenale anticipated the mass-production of the industrial revolution by almost six hundred years. At its peak, this great engine of commerce and war employed 16,000 workers, capable of producing a ship a day. Napoleon destroyed various parts and added others, without ever quite knowing what to do with it, before passing it on to the Austrians who didn't have much idea either. Today, large parts of it serve as exhibition space during the Venice Biennale, but it still effectively functions as a naval base.

A recent initiative had allowed visitors in to see some of the previously inaccessible military areas, as part of a guided tour *al chiaro di luna* - by the light of the moon.

There was already a crowd when we arrived and it immediately transpired that we had a problem, as a German family were the only ones there who didn't speak Italian. It wasn't their fault, it hadn't been advertised as Italian-only, but our guide apologised and said that she didn't speak German. They asked if she could just explain the main bits in English, but - more firmly this time - she declined. Things seemed to be getting off to a fractious start, until Caroline prodded me forward and suggested that I could act as interpreter. The Germans smiled. The guide smiled. I smiled, albeit rather weakly. Still, everyone seemed happy enough with this, so I agreed to give it a go.

As soon as the tour started, however, I realised that this was not going to work. I can't take Italian in and convert it directly into German. I have to mentally translate it into English and then find the German, which is not as easy as it used to be. And by the time I'd done that the conversation had moved on. So, after a few stumbling attempts in a not-entirely-successful Italian/German hybrid, it became obvious that it was easier just to translate into English, letting the anglophone members of the party pass it on to the others.

It's surprising how atmospheric and beautiful a military base can look by the light of the moon. The trouble is, the moonlight by itself wasn't really enough to see everything clearly. It was all quite interesting and, probably, all very fascinating to see -

unfortunately, we just couldn't properly see very much of it. It wasn't made any easier by the fact that the tour had been overbooked and that it was necessary, at times, to walk in single file along unpaved tracks. I would translate as best I could for my German chums, then make my way up the line in order to hear the next bit from the guide and then scurry back in order to pass it on; all of which meant we received a slightly fragmentary description of the place.

It was an enjoyable evening, if harder work than I'd imagined. I wondered if some sort of tip might be forthcoming, but in the end I was happy to settle for their good wishes. An interesting tour, if perhaps better suited for the daylight hours.

Cucina (a little too) Povera

Nervetti. We'd seen these listed occasionally in butcher's shops. We didn't know what they were and it proved difficult to find out. The dictionary translation simply defines them as 'nerves'. Nerves. What do nerves taste like? For that matter what do they look like? They didn't sound like something that needed to be tried in a hurry.

Then Caroline discovered *insalata di nervetti* on sale at the deli counter in *Billa* and decided that we could afford to try 100g of them, just in case. A search on the net showed me that they aren't nerves at all, but a far tastier sounding blend of pressed tendons and meat from a calf's hoof.

Sunday lunchtime arrived, out they came and, well, we both looked at them. A pile of semi-translucent greyish jelly-like cubes. All of a sudden, 100g looked like a bit of a challenge.

Still, it would have been silly to come this far and not give them a go, so we tucked in. I say 'tucked in', but really mean that we half-heartedly prodded around looking for the more appetising bits. I found a small scrap that looked a bit greyer than the others and took this as a sign that it was one of the meatier pieces.

You couldn't actually say they were horrible. You couldn't even say they were particularly unpleasant. They had a mild flavour of onions (unsurprising as they came packaged with a garnish of, well, onions) and not very much else. In fact, if cold slightly-oniony jellyish cubes are your thing, you might find them a bit of a treat.

Cucina Povera - the art of making tasty, nutritious food from the simplest and cheapest of ingredients - is one of Italy's great gifts to the world. The insistence on using every last bit of the animal is commendable. I have winkled a tiny rabbit brain from its skull in a restaurant on Ischia. I have enjoyed crispy sheep brains in the Roman ghetto. I have eaten spleen-in-a-bun in a market in Palermo. This, however, was just a little too *povera*. Neither of us thought we needed to try them again.

A Touch of Grey

Barrow-upon-Soar is not a particularly large village. Nevertheless, I managed to get myself lost in it. Caroline needed some products from Boots and, with the weather playing up, the walk into town was going to make a mess of her hair. So I took the easy Bonus Hubby Points on offer and volunteered to go myself. My new brother-in-law had given me directions: take the first turning right, then the footpath past the school and you'll come to the main street.

Instead of which I found myself in the middle of a housing estate, in a light linen suit just perfect for a Venetian summer and somewhat less so for a wet and windy day in the English Midlands. I took a left and walked along the road for five minutes. Houses. I turned round and went back the way. More houses. I gave up and went back down the footpath and discovered that I had somehow chosen the least obvious of the three I could have taken. I chose the next along and, blessedly, shops appeared. After five minutes shopping I headed back to the house as if setting out for a jaunty stroll along the *Zattere,* past the bemused gaze of the locals kitted out with weatherproof coats and umbrellas, bracing themselves against the icy rain.

Ah, the rain. Proper, cold, wet rain dropping from a slate-grey English sky. I felt ridiculously happy. It was tempting to stretch out on the grass and lie there, being rained on, but it struck me that passers-by might be concerned.

We had returned to the UK for a couple of days to celebrate my sister's wedding and I should have paid more attention to the weather forecast, because we now had just thirty minutes before being pitched into the whole round of buttonholes, photos and welcome drinks. I looked like I'd been dragged backwards through a particularly soggy hedge. I did not look like somebody who ought to be in a wedding photograph.

Caroline spent some time working on my suit with a hairdryer. This used up the Bonus Hubby Points, but at least I was looking vaguely presentable by the time our lift arrived.

It was a warm, cheery and just-boozy-enough affair. Everybody had a good time, my dad made the speech of his life and Helen and Andy looked so happy.

24 hours later we were back home. It seemed strange to be thinking of Venice as home, but, of course, that's what it was now.

Sempre Dritto

In the event of having to ask directions in Venice you will as likely as not be given the answer s*empre dritto* (straight ahead). This translates as 'head in that sort of direction for the next three *campi*, then turn left and cross the first bridge, then take the *calle* on the left or right - doesn't matter which, they should both end up in the same place – and you should be in Campo San Luca, because every walk through San Marco seems to take you through Campo San Luca at some point. And then I think you'll need to ask someone else.'

It's not really an attempt to fob off the tourist, but more that navigating around is so damn complex that you'd forget any proper directions soon enough anyway. And Venice's peculiar geography means that *sempre dritto* will get you to where you want to go. Eventually.

I returned home late from the cinema one evening. Late enough for the men selling bags and the tat merchants to have called it a night, so I was surprised when I turned into Campo Santo Stefano and someone called out 'Excuse me sir...?'

It was a couple in need of directions. They wanted to get to San Marco, but were walking towards the Accademia Bridge. I explained that they were already in the right district, but for the Piazza itself, well, they needed to head in the opposite direction

The young woman complimented me on my English, but her bloke recognised my accent and grinned. 'South Wales, right?' It turned out he was from Wrexham. Now, this would normally be an occasion for manly hugs and perhaps even a spritz, but it was pushing midnight and I really wanted to get home. Sadly, The Only Other Welshman in Venice was also The Unluckiest Welshman in Venice as, of all the people he could have asked for directions, he had asked the man who got lost in Barrow-upon-Soar.

I took a look at their map, pointed out Campo Santo Stefano and Piazza San Marco. I have my own method of getting there, but it's called 'following Caroline' and I wasn't sure I could prod her out of bed at five to midnight and ask her to escort two strangers on their way. I pointed in the general direction and smiled. 'It's *sempre dritto'*, I said.

I hope they made it.

Torcello

Tourists aside, Venice is relatively quiet during August. Those who can manage it head out of town to cooler climes and any number of shops, bars and newspaper stalls have 'closed for holidays' signs on them. Then along comes *Ferragosto* and it becomes even quieter for the day. It was originally a celebration of the middle of summer and the end of hard manual work in the fields, but it also serves as a religious holiday for the Assumption of the Virgin.

Given the number of churches dedicated in some shape or form to the BVM, you'd think this would be the cue for any number of celebrations throughout the city. Oddly, however, they're mainly confined to the remote island of Torcello and its basilica.

Torcello was one of the first islands in the lagoon to be settled. Until the eleventh century it was more powerful than Venice itself, but the island fell into decline as problems with malaria intensified. It lies in the area known, ominously, as the Dead Lagoon.

It seems hard to imagine now, but 20,000 people once lived on Torcello. Today, there are just 11. That's eleven, not eleven thousand. The journey there takes approximately an hour and, once you arrive, a ten minute walk will lead you to what passes for the centre of town; the majority of the mediaeval structures having been scavenged for building materials over the centuries.

What remains is the church of *Santa Fosca*, the *Palazzo dell'Archivio* and the *Palazzo del Consiglio* which together make up the provincial museum; and, most importantly, the Basilica of *Santa Maria Assunta*. A church has stood on this site since the seventh century and was remodelled into its current form around the year 1000. Remodelled in a bit of a hurry as there was a general belief that the world was going to end by the turn of the millennium and they wanted to have it all ready in time.

Where do you start with this building? You could look down, to the mosaic floor; or up to the intricately-sculpted white marble capitals that even impressed the never-knowingly-overwhelmed John Ruskin. But, likely as not, your eye will immediately be drawn to the extraordinary mosaic on the west wall. The Last Judgement. *Ultimo Giudizio.* Or, should you be feeling particularly apocalyptic, the *Doomsday Mosaic.* Christ sits in judgement as the souls of the departed are weighed; whilst those who don't make the cut are prodded downwards into a river of fire by a group of sorrowful-looking angels, to where the Antichrist, sitting on Satan's knee, insouciantly ushers them into Hell, the merest trace of a smile upon his lips.

It's enormous fun (although that presumably wasn't the intention) but the greatest work of art on Torcello, and one of the greatest in all of Venice, is directly opposite. An attenuated mosaic image of the Virgin, alone in the golden space of the apse. This is the *Virgin Theotokos*, the 'God-bearer'; a tall, thin young woman holding the Christ child. Whereas the *Doomsday Mosaic* is all action, this is quiet and powerful in its simplicity. She gazes out at us as if barely controlling an almost unbearable pain; as if she were holding each and every one of us responsible for what is to come.

By contrast, there isn't much in the way of art in the church of Santa Fosca, but it's a calm, cool, reflective space; and, for those with a particular interest in bits of saints, the remains of Santa Fosca and Santa Maura are held in an illuminated case under the altar. We spent about thirty minutes in the archaeological museums and then it was enough of the high culture and time for lunch.

The *Osteria al Ponte del Diavolo* (named for the nearby and less-exciting-than-you-might-think Devil's Bridge) is one of our favourite restaurants in Venice. Caroline had an elegant dish of dressed crab, before moving on to pasta with lobster. I started with a dish of pasta with black truffles, followed by the greatest plate of fried fish in the world, a big crispy pile of vegetable strips, squid, prawns and miscellaneous (and unidentifiable) 'little fish'.

We should perhaps have left it there. At the very least we should have gone for a post-lunch snooze on the comfy looking loungers in the garden. But there was a concert in the Basilica, so we made our way back. However, lunch had been just that little bit *too* leisurely and we found ourselves unable to find a seat with a view. Vivaldi and Boccherini: pleasant enough, but neither of us were in the right mood to properly appreciate it. Ah well. As one quickly learns in Venice, there'll always be more Vivaldi.

I prefer not to dwell on the journey back. Everyone on the island, including the orchestra, seemed to be getting the same boat. Crammed into the *vaporetto*, in steaming thirty-something heat, it resembled a floating Black Hole of Calcutta. But all-in-all, it had been a very good day indeed. Neither of us needed our tea.

San Rocco

Another day, another *festa*, this time for San Rocco, whose *chiesa* is yet another of Venice's Plague Churches. An interesting enough building in itself, although perhaps in need of some TLC; and overshadowed by the adjacent *Scuola Grande*.

The inside of the Scuola itself is almost entirely covered in paintings by Jacopo Tintoretto (with help from his workshop and his son Domenico) who won a competition, in 1564, to decorate the *Sala dell'Albergo*. In fact, he didn't so much win as cheat: the Confraternity had only wanted some initial sketches but Tintoretto found out the exact dimensions required for the ceiling painting, ran up a quick *San Rocco in Glory* and installed it in place. Cue much sucking of teeth and shaking of heads from the judges. This really wasn't the done thing. Tintoretto shrugged and told them that if it was going to be a deal-breaker, well, he might be prepared to let them have it for free.

Cue some swift mental calculations and more shaking of heads. OK, said Tintoretto, I'm cutting my own throat here, but as I've done the centerpiece now, what if I finished off the rest of it - add in a few *allegories*, that sort of thing - and let you have the whole ceiling free, gratis and for nothing?

Hmmm. Well, this was still highly irregular, but nonetheless...the *whole* ceiling, eh? That sounded like a pretty good deal.

So Tintoretto, having 'won' the competition, set to work on the mighty *Crucifixion* that covers one entire wall of the *Sala*, and then moved on to an *Ecce Homo, Christ before Pilate* and a *Road to Calvary* on the opposite wall.

There was no stopping him now. The ceiling of the *Sala Superiore* depicts most of the Book of Exodus and the walls relate the life of Christ. Downstairs, in the *Sala Terrena,* he rattles through the life of the Virgin from Annunciation to Assumption. Now, some of these may not be amongst his *very* best works in Venice (Ruskin himself was lukewarm on a number of them, and particularly disappointed by the rather frumpy Virgin of the *Annunciation*) but the overall effect is overwhelming. If Venice has an equivalent of the Sistine or Scrovegni chapels, it's here.

Entrance was free for the *festa,* together with one of those very serious in-depth Italian tours. Our guide, a *Confratello* himself, took us round every last work, a process that took over two hours. He explained their theological and historical significance in relation to the philosophy of the Confraternity. He digressed in order to discuss their relevance in the context of the Council of Trent (of which, he evidently assumed, we had an in-depth knowledge). And yet, it was all so fascinating we forgot to feel tired and even stopped fretting about the heat.

After covering the entire upper floor, we were shown a couple of works on easel, one by Titian, another by the school of Giorgione. They might have been the standout works in any other space, but, in the midst of all this splendour, we just gave them a cursory glance and a shrug of 'Yeah. Titian.'

Finally, we were finished. We lost a few along the way but nearly all of the group had stuck it out to the very end. The guide smiled and said he'd see us next year. We hoped so.

The Revolution Will Not Be Televised
...because it will be starting later than advertised.

'So what are the Communists up to tonight?' A question we frequently asked ourselves during the *Festa di Liberazione* in Campo San Giacomo dell'Orio, organised by the *Partito della Rifondazione Communista.*

Each evening followed a similar pattern of a political discussion or presentation, followed by some music. A number of stalls sold beer, wine and snacks. Petitions were being signed. T-shirts were sold with the word 'Peace' in a dozen different languages, including Welsh (*Heddwch*, if you're interested).

The first night concerned the plight of workers in a factory in Marghera, where the management were offshoring jobs despite the business turning in good profits. Most of the people around us just seemed to be there for the beer and food, and kept talking throughout, which made it difficult to follow. Still, the following night sounded more interesting, with a play entitled *L'eclisse della Democrazia*, centring around the anti-globalisation G8 demonstrations in Genova in 2001.

Leftie things usually start a bit late. Italian things usually start a bit late. With this in mind, there was probably no need for us to turn up fifteen minutes early, in order to be sure of getting a good seat. As it turned out, with five minutes to go, the audience consisted of ourselves, a man with an iPad and two small boys on bikes, continually circling the seating area like Indians around a wagon train.

The seats slowly filled up over the following 45 minutes, but with no sign of it starting. The man with the iPad must have been beginning to wonder if the battery life really was the advertised ten hours; although the small boys seemed willing and able to keep their circuit going all night if need be.

An hour passed, but was no real hardship. San Giacomo dell'Orio is one of the loveliest squares in Venice and it was a pleasure just to sit around, with the occasional journey to the bar where drinks were being sold at proper comradely prices.

The show finally kicked off, a one-man piece interspersed with music from an accordionist and clarinettist, based around events that Amnesty International have described as '...*the most serious violation of human rights in a Western democracy since the end of World War II.'*

Two hundred thousand demonstrators arrived in Genova in 2001, nearly a hundred of whom were in temporary accommodation in the *Diaz-Pertini* school. Following the discovery of a brace of Molotov cocktails, Italian police stormed the building and turned it into a temporary, illegal, detention centre. Over the course of the night, the protesters were systematically abused and beaten. Sixty were left with serious injuries, three of them comatose. A British journalist was beaten to a bloody pulp. Female detainees were threatened with rape.

The charges against all the detainees at Diaz were ultimately dropped, a judge concluding that they had put up no resistance and that statements had been falsified. The deputy police chief later admitted that the Molotovs had been planted by police in order to justify the raid. 25 officers were convicted of grievous bodily harm and planting evidence. The drawn-out appeals process, together with the statute of limitations in Italian law, means that none of them will go to jail.

The events at Diaz still have resonance in Italy, because it serves as a reminder that - when the wrong people have their hands on the levers of power - it doesn't take much for a liberal Western democracy to behave in a manner that can only be described as fascist.

It's a powerful story that needs to be told and the main actor/performer delivered it well. Unfortunately, the endless musical interludes got in the way and it felt as if their main purpose was to drag a 45 minute show out to 90 minutes. Still, this was the first piece of theatre we'd been to in Venice and it was a good one to start with.

The evening concluded with tango dancing in the *campo*. Almost as soon as the applause had finished, chairs were cleared away and audience members started changing into their dancing shoes. We have vague memories of learning a social foxtrot for our wedding, but decided that this was beyond us; and so we left for the next *vaporetto*, leaving the comrades to tango the night away.

Regata Storica

Caterina Cornaro is perhaps the most significant female figure in Venetian history. In 1468, at the age of 14, she was betrothed to James II of Cyprus; and married him four years later. James died in 1473, leaving his young wife to act as Regent to their infant son. When the younger James died before his first birthday, Caterina was left to rule the kingdom alone, until 1489 when she abdicated in order that Venice might attain complete control of the island. Her return to Venice is marked to this day by the *Corteo Storico* that makes up part of the annual *Regata Storica*.

The *Corteo Storico* puts a cheerier spin on the historical reality: Caterina had not wanted to abdicate, but was forced to do so through a mixture of threats and bribery. Still, Venice - through a cynical but clever and far-sighted piece of *realpolitik* - got what it wanted with control of a strategically important site.

Caterina died in 1510 and is buried in the *Chiesa di San Salvador.* On the Saturday preceding the regatta, as a curtain-raiser to the main event, it hosted a concert in her memory; comprising four variations on the text of *Salve Regina* by Vivaldi, Pergolesi, Handel and Leo. The Pergolesi, in particular, was excellent and it was good to be reminded that there's more to him than the *Stabat Mater.*

There's always a good musical programme at San Salvador. The trouble is, it's an incredibly uncomfortable place to listen to music. The pews hold your back at an awkward angle, almost throwing you forward, and so - if you're above a certain height - you can either sit with your chin resting on your knees, or slouch semi-horizontally, dangling your feet under the pew in front. Still, there are two excellent Titians (the *Transfiguration* and the *Annunciation*) and a fake Bellini to take your mind off things.

Sunday was the day of the *Regata* itself. We made a quick circuit of possible viewing points along the Grand Canal, but nothing seemed quite satisfactory. In the end we took some deckchairs along to Campo San Samuele, along with reading material and wine with which to while away the afternoon.

The *Corteo Storico* passed by, representing the entrance of Caterina and the Doge, followed by any number of historic-looking barges, then locals in various degrees of period costume, rowing clubs and...well, anybody who had a boat who fancied joining in. After the *Corteo*, the *Regata* proper began, consisting of races for different age groups and classes of boat. It was impressive to watch, although obviously of greater interest to those with a serious interest in rowing.

Yes, it may play fast-and-loose with history, but that doesn't really matter. It was a very pleasant way to spend the afternoon. The weather played fair with us, a layer of cloud keeping the sun off without ever threatening to rain.

Dinner was a fine piece of tuna marinated in gin and red wine. An unusual combination of flavours, due to my mistake in assuming that *ginevra* translated as gin and not juniper. I still think it worked.

Mussels

The Film Festival finished without us ever really being aware that it had been on at all. Oh yes, there was coverage in the press every day; but, unless you go out to the Lido, it's not inescapable in the same way as the Biennale of Art. It may not have *quite* the glamour of Cannes, but there was a general feeling that it had been a good year, with a strong, serious programme.

I used to be obsessed with cinema, but don't seem to have the time these days. Twenty years ago I'd have been in a frenzy of excitement at the thought of being on the doorstep of one of the world's major film events and then, when it finally happened, I hardly noticed it.

Still, it wasn't the only festival in town, as the great and the good of *la settima arte* found themselves competing for the public's affections with the Alberoni Festival of Mussels (or, in Veneziano, the *Festa della Peocio*). The Venetian ability to turn anything into a *Festa* is an admirable one, whether it be for Artichokes, Mussels or Revolutionary Communism.

It was a cheery if low-key affair - there is, after all, a limit to how much of a celebration you can build around a mollusc. There was a bouncy castle and football for the kids, and bands playing in the evening; but it was mainly an excuse to eat lots of mussels and none the worse for that.

More seriously, it's run in conjunction with the World Wildlife Fund to raise awareness of the complex ecosystem of the lagoon and the Alberoni dunes; and, specifically, their efforts in sea turtle conservation. I had no idea there even were sea turtles in that area of the Adriatic.

When we got home I took down a recently acquired cookbook, that fell open at a recipe for turtle soup. This really wasn't what I wanted to think about following an afternoon of reading about the exploits of cheery cartoon turtles. We had stuffed squid for dinner instead.

Work

Early one Wednesday morning. Earlier than I'd been used to for some time, at any rate. I stopped off at my regular newspaper stand, stuck my copy of *Repubblica* into my laptop case and walked to Rialto. It was quiet, hardly anyone on the bridge yet, but the *vaporetti* were starting to fill up and I found myself sitting amongst a group of excited Japanese tourists. I read my paper and obstinately refused to look at the view as we made our way up the Grand Canal. This was silly, obviously, but I was making a statement: 'I can look at this any time, but right now something important is going on in the world that I need to know about. Because I am not on holiday, oh no, I am going to work, just like any ordinary Venetian.'

I was pleased at having secured some work teaching Business English in Venice itself, although it was a little deflating when it turned out to be in Tronchetto; a part of the city so resolutely un-magical it even has cars. Still, it was convenient to travel to, so I couldn't complain. And the job had come so completely out of the blue, it hadn't left me time to be nervous: *'Can you take over from another teacher? Great. Can you start on Wednesday...no we don't have anything to hand over to you...sorry, but you'll have to wing it for the first lesson or so.'*

The hours passed with no disasters to speak of. Everyone seemed pleased and I even enjoyed it. I made my way back to the *vaporetto* stop, took a coffee in a local bar and read more of the paper. I stopped off at the Rialto market on the way home and picked up four *seppie* for tea, a bargain at just a couple of euros. I noticed the water was higher than it had been for a while and some of the *calli* were starting to flood; a sign that autumn was coming.

I hopped on the next boat, bag of cuttlefish in one hand and laptop in the other. This time, I looked at the view and - at that moment - felt more than ever that I truly belonged here.

LiberArti

Art or Shed?

Let me explain. A few Biennales ago, we were wandering around one of the off-site exhibitions and came across a room full of junk. Tools, bits of lumber, rubbish; that sort of thing. And, with our brains addled by two weeks of intensive contemporary art, we couldn't make our minds up if it was Art. Or just a Shed. We eventually decided it was just a Shed (I'm still not 100% sure that we were right) and, ever since, 'Art or Shed' has been our Occam's Razor for those difficult 'yes, but is it *art*?' questions.

The Architecture Biennale was by now in full swing, but we'd yet to pay much attention to it. Not through lack of interest, but there simply hadn't been enough time as other, more immediate, events kept getting in the way.

One of these was *LiberArti,* a free arts festival running over three days on Giudecca. It's very much a community affair. There were no grand parties for celebrities - the opening ceremony was just a ceremonial hanging of a home-made banner over the Ponte Lungo.

As you might expect from the name, everything was free. The bigger events were linked with the Biennale and not really part of LiberArti at all, but when you put them together they made Giudecca one big, long art crawl. It took in almost every kind of space. Some were just shops hosting a couple of pictures in the window. There were exhibitions in professional galleries, in *palazzi*, in a working men's club, in artists' studios, in the hall of somebody's house. There was also performance art, theatre and a screening of *Don't Look Now* (which has the splendid Italian title of *Un Dicembre Rosso Shocking*) - all of which we managed to miss, for reasons of geography and time.

It wasn't all brilliant. Some of it was just enthusiastic amateur level. But that didn't matter. What was important was the way it engaged people. People in gallerics were eager to talk and there was a real feeling of community about the whole thing. We kept running into one of the organisers (Andrea, a splendid chap from the excellent Bar Palanca) who was always keen to recommend places to us.

As we made our way around, crossing off exhibitions on the map, we came across an abandoned headboard sporting a sad little row of fairy lights. We stopped and stared at it for a while. There was supposed to be some art in this spot, but could this really be it? In short, was it Art? Or just a Shed?

I'd been unable to make my mind up about Giudecca. It's a strange mixture of styles: typical Venetian buildings mix with modern blocks of flats and some slightly shabbier parts. I'd never been able to decide if I liked it or not. But at the end of three days of *LiberArti* I decided I'd done it a disservice. Yes, it has its less attractive areas, but there's also a real feeling of 'localness' here. It's Venice, but not quite as we know it, and much nicer than I'd thought.

Outlying Islands

2012 was the second annual *Isole in Rete* in which the public get the chance to visit some of the normally inaccessible islands of the north lagoon; whilst some of the others, on the regular transport network, host special events.

First up on our itinerary was *San Giacomo in Paludo* (or, if you prefer, St James-in-the-Marsh). This is a tiny wee spit of an island, not on any *vaporetto* route. It went through the usual cycle of many of the smaller, abandoned islands: monastery, dissolution, gunpowder store and rack-and-ruin. Like many of them, it is now being looked after by the equivalent of the National Trust.

There isn't very much to see here now. Little remains of the monastery itself, the powder magazines are ruined; and many of the buildings are in a dangerous condition due to the continual effect of *moto ondoso*, and are therefore inaccessible. Nevertheless, it's nice that people think enough of the importance of preserving the place to give up their time and energy to look after it.

Mazzorbetto was next - technically an island in itself, although separated by only a few feet from the main body of Mazzorbo. The fort, an early 20th Century structure, served as a fascist holiday camp during the Mussolini era. It then fell into ruin for fifty years, before being taken over by the Boy Scout movement. Annoyingly, we'd already gone for a mediocre lunch on Torcello, whereas we'd have been better off coming straight to Mazzorbetto and having the scouts grill us some sausages. A photographic exhibition recorded the history of the island during the 20th century. Images of hundreds of happy, smiling families from the 1920s, in what would be nothing more than nostalgic period photographs were it not for the presence of banners that simply read *Grazie, Duce*.

Frustratingly, Mazzorbo was no more than ten feet away across a canal, but this was still enough to compel us to wait for the next boat. It briefly crossed my mind that, if I just took a good run up, I could make it to the other side. Then I got a mental image of the consequences of *not* making it and decided waiting was the better option. My long-jumping years are long behind me, if, indeed, they were ever there at all.

Sant'Erasmo, of course, is on a standard route, but we stopped there anyway for an exhibition at the *Torre Massimiliano*, an imposing structure built when the Austrians were in charge.

It's typically used as an exhibition space these days; and was hosting a photographic display of fortified structures throughout Venice and the surrounding area. Unfortunately there were few captions, with the result that it didn't take long before one photograph of a crumbling ruin started to resemble every other photograph of a crumbling ruin. We then failed to find any sign of a supposed vineyard tour near the *vaporetto* stop and left, thinking that it hadn't been worth the detour.

This left us short of time, as we had to get back to Venice, grab a bite to eat and then catch a boat out to Lazzaretto Nuovo for an evening concert. We just had time for a spectacularly underwhelming pizza at a restaurant on the *Fondamente Nuove*, where even the waiter seemed embarrassed and looked at us as if to say, 'Yeah. I know.'

There was an almighty queue at the stop and not enough space for everyone on the boat. Still, the organisers had anticipated this and laid on an extra service which arrived ten minutes later. It was dark by the time we arrived, but the island was illuminated by a strip of citronella candles which served to light the path to the *lazzaretto* itself and to keep the clouds of mosquitoes at bay.

Crowds of people stood around, chatting and wondering what to do next, and then everyone gradually began to fall silent. Because something magical was happening. Slowly, a boat emerged from the darkness and from across the water, barely perceptible at first, came the sound of a choir. They disembarked and – still singing - lead us along the candlelit path and into the hall.

It was a wonderful concert of sacred and profane music, from Gabrieli and Palestrina right up to the present day, taking in some enjoyably unexpected material along the way (John Dowland's *Fine Knacks for Ladies* in Italian accents). It turned out that one of the basses was also in the same choir as me. I asked him afterwards how on earth he found time to be in two of them. Oh, he shrugged, tonight's concert hadn't taken much rehearsing so it was no trouble to fit in. Which was remarkable given the quality of the singing.

We needn't have bothered with the disappointing pizza, as a buffet and drinks had been laid on for everyone afterwards. The evening ended on a downbeat note, however, when one grumpy-arsed member of the audience kicked up a fuss about having to pay for his ticket home. The organiser did his best to point out that - given that he had enjoyed a free concert and supper – paying for transport was perhaps not *that* iniquitous; but Mr Grumpy was having none of it and paid up with very bad grace. Personally, I'd have left him there to stew until the next boat arrived, which could have been anything up to a week, competing for the island's scant food resources with the suspiciously well-fed looking cats. A slightly sour end, then, to an otherwise fine day.

The Isle of the Dead

Isole in Rete day 2, started with a visit to *Tenuta Scarpa* on Mazzorbo, an *agriturismo* project centring around the ideas of environmental education and organic agriculture. The holding includes a hostel, a smart-looking hotel and restaurant, and (and this was the real selling point for us) a vineyard. As part of the weekend's events, they'd arranged a series of one-hour guided tours.

Except it didn't quite work out that way. What actually happened is that we turned up and stood by a pond for 15 minutes whilst one of the guides explained the project to us. And that was it. Yes, it all seemed very worthy and deserving of support, but I couldn't help thinking *we got up early on Sunday morning to come out here and stand in a field and - crucially - we are not even going to get to try the wine!*

We were left to our own devices after that and took a wander around the vineyard. It was pleasant enough but felt like a walk around a biscuit factory without being able to eat any biscuits.

The afternoon was more successful, as we took a boat tour to the very outer reaches of the lagoon. North-east of Torcello lies the island of Sant'Ariano. The bone island. The official cemetery of San Michele had limited space so, following ten years' interment, your remains would be exhumed and deposited on the ossuary island instead. If you were a normal inhabitant of Venice, this was where you finally ended up.

It isn't used any more and it's impossible to see what lies beyond the walls as it's completely overgrown. There's a tiny chapel (I could make out a crucifix but little else) and a jetty, with a warning sign advising that landing is strictly forbidden. The reasons are unclear, but I think the stonework is now crumbling and dangerous. Or is that just what they want us to think?

I would dearly love to have a closer look but it doesn't seem to be possible. Perhaps it's better left to the imagination anyway.

We headed further out, to the far reaches of the northern lagoon. Tiny scraps of land, long since pillaged for their stonework. On an island consisting of little more than a ruined house, a battered sign read 'No Hunting'. The overriding impression was one of silence and desolation. Then I turned 180°, towards the airport, and the illusion was shattered. But, for a moment, this had felt like the very end of the line.

Scarpa

The *Fondazione Querini* Stampalia hosted a number of events and exhibitions for the architecture biennale. Most of these were only of modest interest to us; nevertheless, it's always a pleasure to visit here. The real attraction, for ourselves at least, is the architecture of Carlo Scarpa; without doubt, the most important Venetian architect of the 20th century. I'm embarrassed to admit that we hadn't heard of him before we became regular visitors to Venice, yet we'd encountered his work without even being aware of it. Indeed, if you've spent any time here or in Florence you've almost certainly seen examples of his architecture: he remodelled the space that holds the three great *Maeste* by Giotto, Cimabue and Duccio in the Uffizi; and renovated the picture galleries of both the Museo Correr and Accademia in Venice.

Spend some time with his work and you begin to understand why Luigi Nono lauded him as *'the architect of infinite possibilities.'* His buildings are rarely flashy examples of 'superstar' architecture, but his work, and his influence, is to be found throughout the city. The Olivetti showroom that he designed as a calling card for the company is a hidden gem, lying almost unnoticed off Piazza San Marco. The ground floor of the *Querini Stampalia* was remodelled by him in the early 1950s and is, for my money, one of the most thrilling interiors in all Venice.

Head out to the *giardini* and you'll see his monument to the women partisans. Within the gardens themselves are his ticket booth for the Biennale, the pavilion of Venezuela and the sculpture court of the central pavilion. Scarpa-influenced staircases and windows are a *leitmotif* in the city's modern, or remodelled, buildings.

If you only had a couple of days to spend here, you could choose to completely ignore the more traditional sites and build an itinerary solely around its modern architecture. That might seem almost wilfully perverse, but I think it would actually be a deeply cool thing to do.

La Festa del Mosto

Early autumn, and an alarming number of festivals were passing us by. *Venezia citta viva* and the *Settimana culturale nell'isola per la citta* had come and gone, and even 'Extreme', the contemporary music biennale, had finished without us finding the time to see anything.

Still, the Festival of Artichokes had proved an unexpected success, so we decided to trog along to Sant'Erasmo's *Festa del Mosto* (or the festival of wine must: the unfermented grape juice produced by the pressing - or treading - of grapes).

Sant'Erasmo gets busy on these sorts of occasions, so we made sure to be up early on Sunday morning to get the boat from *Fondamente Nuove*. Sure enough, the *vaporetto* was packed, but getting there 30 minutes in advance paid off and at least we got seats. So far, so good, until we reached the *Cappanone* stop (one before *Chiesa*, which is where the Festa was taking place) and the conductor announced to a disgruntled boat load of people that, in spite of what the timetable might have said, this was the end of the line. So everyone disembarked and began the long trek to the *chiesa*.

It was an unusually hot day for October and we had no idea

how long the walk was likely to be. After fifteen minutes or so we toyed with the idea of giving up and turning back, but we couldn't tell if we'd gone more than halfway. A young woman on a bicycle passed us in the opposite direction. A few minutes later she passed us again. I considered offering her money for her bike, but feared the gesture might be misinterpreted.

We walked for about 30 minutes until, upon rounding a corner, we saw the welcome sight of the church directly ahead of us. A less welcome sight was that of a boat, in defiance of what we'd been told, steaming up to the jetty.

It had been a waste of time getting up early and we'd had a wasted walk as well, but hopefully the Festa would make up for it. And it was, well, OK-ish. Lunch was pleasant enough. There were a few stalls selling local produce. There were also some small children treading grapes (I think they were volunteers rather than their parents having had them put to work in the fields) but grape-treading isn't a tremendously visual experience and after 30 seconds or so you've pretty much got the idea.

We took a brief look around the church (no great art to look at, but quite interesting for its fascist-period facade), bought a bottle of red wine *mosto* and decided we may as well go home.

We stood in line at the *Chiesa* stop for ten minutes or so, caught the next *vaporetto* and settled into our seats. It had been a disappointing day but at least the boat wasn't too crowded.

Five minutes later the conductor announced that the service was terminating at *Cappanone*. We were disgorged onto the jetty into a seething crowd of people waiting for the next boat to Venice. We should all have moved to the back of the queue but nobody was going to do that in case they failed to get on, and the sheer weight of numbers made it impossible anyway. The result was a group, myself included, braced precariously on the edge of the jetty. If anyone behind tried to move forward, or even sneezed vigorously, I would end up in the lagoon.

The next boat arrived, but the captain didn't want to pull up to the mooring as he was afraid - with good reason - that somebody would get pushed in and be crushed between the jetty and the boat. He kept shouting for us to move back, but nobody wanted to lose their space and it was impossible to get the crowd behind us to shift even an inch. At one point it looked like he'd given up in disgust and was going to leave us all there but, finally, he reversed in as slowly as he could. The conductor then tried to get us to make way for the people getting off, but nobody could move. It took an age to get everybody out and both the captain and conductor looked severely pissed off. It wasn't their fault but ACTV had fouled up badly by not taking account of the likely extra number of passengers.

We got back to the city and went for a consolation beer at *La Cantina*. Inevitably, it was closed. It had all been a bit like hard work with nothing to show for it except 1.5 litres of red wine must. Which, splendidly, ended up saving the day. It was a very pleasant sweet wine, just perfect as an after-dinner drink and it made a delicious red wine sauce for a roast duck as well. I'm not saying I'd rush back to the next agricultural festival on Sant' Erasmo (at one point I swore I wouldn't go back there even if Barenboim was conducting the Ring Cycle), but, just maybe, it was worth the trouble after all.

Benedetto Marcello

Caroline has always wondered why I don't sing more around the house. The answer is partly that I feel a little self-conscious (although the neighbours round here are likely to be a more sympathetic audience than they ever were in Leith); but mainly that repeating difficult sections over and over again is going to become annoying, especially if it's a piece she doesn't like. I suppose it's unlikely that I'll ever be cast as Mozart's Queen of the Night, but, if I were, I think I would just have to check into a hotel for a couple of weeks. So even if there's a performance coming up I tend to concentrate on revising the score instead of singing out loud.

Which brings me to *Cantori Veneziani* and my first concert with them - Leonard Bernstein's *Chichester Psalms* and Benedetto Marcello's setting of Psalm 36. I am afraid to say that I had never heard of Marcello before (more than a little embarrassing as we live two minutes' walk from the *Conservatorio* that bears his name) but he turns out to have been one of the most interesting figures in Venetian musical history. Composer, lawyer and politician, he served on Venice's Council of Forty, acted as governor of the city of Pola (now Pula in Croatia) and *camerlengo* of Brescia; and still found time to compose hundreds of works. Amongst these is the *Estro Poetico-Armonico*, based on the text of the first fifty psalms and regarded as his greatest work.

Marcello, himself the subject of a long-forgotten opera by Joachim Raff, is an obscure figure in the UK. Perhaps it's little wonder I'd never heard of him, as there's very little of his music commercially available. And that's a great shame because, on the evidence of Psalm 36, he deserves to be much better known beyond the lagoon. It's an absolutely gorgeous piece.

The week running up to the performance was a hectic one. There were the regular Monday and Thursday rehearsals, with an extra four hours in the concert hall - nothing less than the Scuola Grande di San Rocco - on the Friday night; and a final *prova* two hours before the concert on Saturday. But it wasn't just the music that needed to be sorted out, oh no...

Dress code for this sort of thing in the UK is always straightforward: evening dress (or *uno smoking*) and bow tie. Not in Italy. In fact, they find the very idea amusing, as if the Brits really do still dress as if they were in *Downton Abbey*. Gianfranco told me he bought a *smoking* thirty years ago and has worn it twice. No, dress code - for the men at least - turned out to be more complicated than that. On Monday, we were told to wear black trousers, black shirts and the regulation orange tie. On Tuesday, this had changed to a black suit and white shirt. By Wednesday, the black shirt was back in vogue; and by Thursday it was being matched with a black jacket. At the rehearsal on Friday everybody decided it was too hot to wear a jacket at all, so black trousers, black shirt and orange tie it was. Of course, this meant that - should anybody have needed to go out and buy any of the elements - they only had half a day in which to do so. This might explain why Max wore a striped blue shirt on the night itself and Stefano turned up in his jeans.

I had to fight the impulse to laugh out loud at the sheer absurdity of it all. An ex-computer programmer from Swansea, singing a work by an obscure Venetian composer in a room full of Tintorettos? This was *insane*!

The concert itself was practically sold out. Seven hundred seats, nearly all taken, a good result on a night that had a number of rival concerts throughout the city (it was the first performance of the Marcello in modern times, which helped). Now, usual protocol for classical concerts is to give the audience the 'difficult' piece first and then finish with something less challenging (the musical equivalent of a reward for eating your greens); but the Bernstein is extremely hard on the voice and had to be last. So Marcello was first, then Bernstein, with an encore of the final chorus of the Marcello to send everyone home with a warm glow.

It all went very well and everyone seemed pleased. There was a party afterwards; much wine was drunk and enormous pizzas were consumed. People were keen to ask me what I thought of the concert, about singing in such an extraordinary space and what a shame it was that I didn't get to wear my *smoking*. It was another occasion in which I felt that little bit more at home.

Caroline was still up when I got back. She thought we sounded wonderful and that the Marcello was lovely.

'And the Bernstein?'

'Like being hit around the head with a sock filled with wet sand.'

I shrugged. Fair enough, it's a piece that divides people.

'But it's fantastically exciting to sing', I added, and launched into LA! MA! LA MA! *Lamah rag'shu...lamah rag'shu goyim, lamah rag'shu?*

I saw her pained expression, and stopped.

'Too much?'

She nodded.

And that, dear reader, is the reason I don't sing at home.

Acqua (properly) Alta

The alarm went off at 7am on Saturday morning. The long wail of a siren, followed by a succession of 'pleeps'. Two tones, this time, indicating that the high tide would be bringing *acqua alta* up to a height of around 120 cm above the norm. This would be the highest we'd yet experienced. Thus far the most dramatic thing we'd seen had been a man removing his shoes and socks prior to doggedly wading through an unexpected lake in the vicinity of the *Carmini;* but 120cm was high enough to affect us directly.

Caroline had signed us up to all sorts of email/text warnings and had double-checked the news and the tide tables (there is something pretty cool about living somewhere where you need to check the tides). I'd dropped our *paratia* into place the night before. I had no great faith in its flood-preventing qualities given that the rubber seal around the outside was perished, but it was worth a go.

The street was starting to properly flood by the time Caroline was on her second cup of tea. I took a look downstairs to see how the barrier was faring. As well as I expected. The level of water in the hall might have been a quarter-centimetre less than outside, but that was a moot point as it had reached the staircase anyway.

Caroline went out to do the shopping whilst I stayed behind to clean the flat. As I watched her splash her way down the street, carrying her trolley above the water level, it struck me that a morning in a warm, dry flat with the radio on was the better deal, vacuuming or no.

The waters subsided after a few hours. It hadn't really been all that dramatic. Yes, a number of streets were flooded. Yes, a number of tourists had had to resort to emergency footwear (black bin-liners seem a popular alternative). But most of the *vaporetti* were able to keep running, shops stayed open and people went about their business. It wasn't long before everything was back to normal.

The first acqua alta of the season tends to make the UK papers, because it makes for a good picture. The *Daily Telegraph* covered it in near-apocalyptic terms, with a headline reading 'High tide brings chaos to Venice as acqua alta swamps St Marks Square'. However Piazza San Marco is the lowest point in Venice and is always the first to be hit with flooding. A square full of paddling tourists is not 'chaos'. It's how the city works.

Return of the Crabs
They're back - and this time they're armoured!

Caroline returned from the market with a bag of small crabs, or, to give them their Venetian name, *masanette*. Remember the soft-shelled *moeche*? Well, these are the same, only later in the season, all female and tooled up with hard shells and proper claws.

They were a more active bunch than the soft-shelled guys. I gave them a rinse under running water and within seconds three of them had made a break for it, over the edge of the sieve and into the sink. I gently plopped them back into, shall we say, 'the waiting room' with the aid of a teaspoon: they may have been small, two inches across at most, but their claws were big enough to get an 'Ow!' out of our fishmonger when she bagged them up.

The recommended cooking method is to put them in a pan of cold water and bring it to the boil. I wasn't all that happy about this (I don't imagine the crabs were over the moon either) but it seemed to dispatch them quickly, long before the water became properly hot.

Then the real work began. I took the first crab, removed the legs and claws, levered off the top shell and then painstakingly excised the 'Dead Men's Fingers' with my smallest, sharpest knife. I then repeated the process for the other two dozen or so. I laid the halves out on a plate and dressed them with salt, pepper, lemon and parsley. The mixture of the deep red-bronze crab shells, the bright yellow roe and the green of the parsley made for a very pretty dish.

So what are they like? Well, they're *quite* nice, but there's such a tiny amount of meat to be winkled out of the shells that I'm not sure the ratio of 'Eating Pleasure' versus 'Sheer Amount of Arsing Around' is really worth it. Worth trying, although I wasn't sure I could see them becoming a staple.

Rain

The weather forecast suggested that winter was on its way, so we decided to visit the Architecture Biennale pavilions at the *Giardini* while it was still relatively dry.

Like the visual art biennale, it's a mixed bag. Greece, Poland, Finland and, particularly, Romania were excellent. The Brazilians thoughtfully provided a room full of hammocks for the weary architecture hound to relax in and a selection of guitars to strum away on. It is an immutable scientific law that every man of a certain age will attempt to play *Smoke on the Water* if left in the presence of a guitar for more then five minutes. And, yes, this did happen.

Elsewhere, the Russians and Czechs were relying too heavily on iPad-related gimmickry. The USA pavilion was well-meant, but they didn't seem to have made much of an effort. The Cypriots provided an indoor beach, the Belgians were intimidatingly highbrow and the Dutch installation had broken down altogether.

As we made our way back to the *vaporetto* stop, it started to rain. Proper rain. It rained and rained and rained and rained and rained. Rain of Biblical proportions. Rain of Scottish proportions. It carried on for the whole weekend.

There was a performance of Mozart's *Requiem* that Sunday evening, at the church of San Trovaso. We'd been stuck in the house all day, but if it hadn't been an opportunity to hear the one work by Mozart that Caroline actually likes, we wouldn't have bothered. We kitted ourselves out in coats, hats and wellington boots and splashed our way to the Sant'Angelo stop, only to see the *vaporetto* pulling away from the jetty. Maintenance had been going on at this pontoon for months, leaving it without walls and unprotected from the elements. The rain verged on the horizontal and waiting for the next boat would leave us soaked through. Another 'can we be arsed?' moment but, given that we'd come this far, we decided to press on and walk.

We arrived a good thirty minutes early to find the church already busy and the choir halfway through the *Sanctus*. For a second we thought we'd got the time wrong and they were about to finish; which would almost, but not quite, have been funny. Then we discovered it was still the rehearsal and they'd let people in to get out of the rain.

San Trovaso always feels to me as if it needs a little money and TLC. There are two works by Tintoretto, notably the *Temptation of St Anthony*, where Ruskin's attention was caught by the figure of a woman who 'might be taken for a very respectable person, but that there are flames playing around her loins'; although, despite my best efforts, I've never been able to make out any loins at all, flaming or otherwise.

The concert itself was well-enough played and well-enough sung, but the lack of male voices in the choir was painfully evident. The *Dies Irae* and *Confutatis* were far too well-mannered, when they need to sound like the very end of the world. The encore was also unnecessary. It was in a good cause (restoration funds) and got us out of the house, but, in real life at least, there are no encores after a requiem.

Acqua (extremely) Alta

Early one Wednesday evening, I found myself making my way back home from a class on the Lido. It was pitch dark, with a howling wind sweeping in from the lagoon and pushing great sheets of water along the streets. It was only 7:30 in the evening, but there was not another soul to be seen. No-one with any sense was venturing outdoors. I knew the tiny umbrella in my bag wouldn't last more than a couple of seconds in the gale, so I crammed my hat onto my head as best I could and headed for the bus shelter as fast as a man in a pair of wellies can run.

Caroline texted me to say she'd seen tourists on a gondola back in the *centro storico*. The rain was horizontal. You could hardly see beyond a few metres. You would have to be insane to want to do this. But our Japanese cousins are made of sterner stuff. They'd come this far to have a gondola ride and, by God, they were damn well going to have one even if it nearly killed them.

A bus arrived within a couple of minutes and then there was a short wait for a *vaporetto* from Santa Maria Elisabetta. For once, nobody wanted to go and wait on the jetty in order to be first in line for a seat. Instead everyone huddled under cover until the very last moment. A few young people were in fancy dress, evidently on their way to a Halloween party. I hope it was worth it. It would have needed to have been the best party in the world.

I squelched back into the flat forty minutes later. Our landlady had been round to put a new seal on the *paratia* which now seemed to be properly chocked into place. Caroline, bless her, had been cooking, and a steaming risotto of gorgonzola and walnut, with copious quantities of wine, soon had me feeling human again.

There was no point in even thinking about going out in this, so we had an early night. There was a code red warning for *acqua alta* with the peak, at midnight, predicted at 140 cm above average. Our street was still flooded the next morning; the water levels kept high by a combination of the phase of the moon, the incoming scirocco and a lagoon already swollen by days of rain.

I needed to go out and buy a loaf of bread. It was the first of November - *Ognissanti* or All Saints' Day, a public holiday – and the city was relatively quiet. I splashed my way to Campo Santo Stefano and then along the *passerelle* to the supermarket where, for a few minutes, everything seemed normal. Then back outside, to the flooding, pedestrians in disposable waterproof boots and shopkeepers running pumps or sweeping out the pools of water as best they could.

Venice had remained relatively unaffected by *acqua alta* during the previous year, the water level rarely exceeding 110cm above the average. This, however, was the most sustained flooding for nearly fifty years. A third of the city was affected for fifteen hours, the longest period since 1966.

The water levels have been higher, sometimes much higher, in the past. Ominously, however, half of the highest recorded levels have occurred in the past decade. The MOSE project may help - great submerged gates that can be raised in order to isolate the lagoon in the event of exceptionally high waters - but nobody seems 100% convinced and there's no sign of it being finished any day soon.

You might have seen pictures on television of tourists 'swimming' in Piazza San Marco. If you've walked through the piazza and seen what tends to litter it, you might think twice about walking barefoot, let alone swimming. Still, I hear they can do marvellous things with antibiotics these days.

Again, from the news reports in the UK, you might have assumed that something truly apocalyptic was happening. If you spoke to local people, the reaction was more phlegmatic: wear wellies and don't go near Piazza San Marco. It wasn't 'chaos', it wasn't a 'disaster' and, no, Venice is not about to slip beneath the waves.

The reality, of course, is that you couldn't *really* swim in the piazza. The water was deep, yes, but not as much as all that. The real, serious problems were not in Venice but elsewhere throughout Northern Italy. Three electricity workers were killed when a bridge collapsed in Grosseto. But sadly this was never going to be as newsworthy as an image of tourists sitting around in their swimming costumes outside a cafe. It's November. It's cold. For God's sake put some trousers on.

Becoming a Leghista

I was waiting for a bus home from Mestre when a guy came bounding past, gave me a smile that could best be described as ambiguous, briefly jabbed a finger in my direction and cried *'Lega Nord!'* I was, as you might imagine, taken aback by this, and he was on his way without even breaking his stride by the time I manage to splutter out a *'Certamente no!'*

The *Lega Nord,* in case you don't know, are the separatist party of Northern Italy. Their platform is that the south of the country is corrupt and crime-ridden and everyone in the north would be better off if they were to secede and form an independent state called *Padania.* They have, at best, a modest amount of support; nevertheless, this has been enough to keep them in government, as minor partners of Berlusconi, for much of the past twenty years.

Opinion on the Northern League varies. Some see them as an eclectic group of individuals from right across the political spectrum who genuinely believe that they are culturally so very different from the south that the only logical way forward is separation. Others consider them an unpleasant bunch of neo-fascists. Now, I'm trying to be objective about this, but given their obsession with an invented past (*Padania* has never existed except in the broadest geographical sense), weird symbolism (the *Carroccio*, a mobile altar that could be wheeled into battle), a dubious attitude to foreign people (their ex-leader's suggestion that the illegal immigration problem on Lampedusa could be solved if only the navy were allowed to open fire on unarmed refugees) and genuine 100% mentalism (their high-profile MEP who expressed support for Anders Breivik and attempted to set fire to a homeless man)...well, you'll understand if I'm erring towards the 'fascist bastards' side.

Now, I happen to have a long bright green scarf that I bought for a St Patrick's Day party a few years ago. Long enough to do that 'folding in two and looping through itself' thing, and not so chunky that it stopped my head moving. It resembled a big floppy cravat. But the thing about the Northern League is that they're very big on green. Green flags. Green shirts. And bright green scarves...

I'm not sure what the man at the bus stop actually meant. Was he an actual *Leghista* (in which case, was I supposed to give him a clenched-fist salute?), an anti-fascist (in which case a clenched-fist salute might have been met with a bunch of fives), or, more likely, did he just see my scarf and pick up on it for a joke?

At any rate, it was packed away and another was pressed into service. A shame. I was rather fond of my long green scarf. But not so much that I was prepared to risk dangling from it.

Part 5

Work

Work came in steadily, as if being in work was the best way of generating it.

We had started out by emailing literally every language school we could find on the internet. Of course, we had no real knowledge of the education sector to speak of and had to try and big up our 'life experience' in the hope of making our wafer-thin teaching CVs appear more impressive than they were.

Most of these emails went unanswered. A school in Treviso replied, but lost interest when they found out that we were living in Venice. The travelling, they told me, would be too difficult for us. I had naively assumed that we would be working a standard 9 to 5 day. It wasn't going to be like that – work would be split between morning sessions in schools and evening sessions for adult learners. Of course, I should have thought of this – there is, after all, a reason why 'evening classes' are called 'evening classes'.

This made it more difficult than expected. I had thought it would be straightforward enough to commute from Venice to Treviso or Padua. I now realised this wasn't going to be possible.

Caroline was the first of us to find paid work, with a small language school on the Lido. She started with a pair of Ukrainian women, one of whom spoke some English and the other of whom spoke some Italian. After the first lesson, one of them demanded to be taught in Italian. After the second, the other demanded to be taught in English. There was no third lesson and the same students got through three other teachers by Christmas.

This turned out to be a stroke of good fortune, however, as within a couple of weeks she found herself employed by a reputable private language school in Mestre.

I'd found some short-term business contracts, but they were coming to an end. It was now up to me to cobble together enough part-time work to ensure we could bring in a living wage.

The Blackboard Jungle

We taped a spreadsheet to our fridge. That might not sound like very much, but it felt significant. By now the two of us were working something that approximated a full week and we needed to keep track of where we were.

Caroline was working as a teaching assistant in Mestre; whilst I had become the very definition of a peripatetic teacher with classes in Tronchetto and Marghera, and a growing number of individual lessons on the side.

'No job too small' was a useful motto. From a financial point of view, it made no sense at all to travel to the Lido and back for a single 90 minute lesson. But I picked up more and more classes on the back of that and reasonable money was now starting to come in.

I had the easier introduction to teaching. My students included a keen-as-mustard water taxi driver; a nice lady who worked at *La Fenice*; and a lovely bloke who ran a fine art restoration business and wanted to spend his second lesson discussing a short story by Chekov.

Caroline, by contrast, had to deal with classes packed full of shouty, hyperactive Italian teenagers, hopped up on a deadly cocktail of caffeine, e-numbers and hormones.

I considered myself extremely fortunate to have avoided this fate until I found myself with the chance of a contract in nearby Spinea. Just a few hours a week, but, like the job on the Lido, there was always the possibility of it developing into something more substantial. Teaching middle-school children for a couple of hours on Monday and Friday afternoons.

'So, basically being a teaching assistant?', I asked.

'Erm, not exactly. You see, the school day finishes at 1pm. You'll be taking after-school classes on your own.'

'Hang on, you mean there's not going to be an actual teacher there *at all*!?'

'No, just you. But they should be fine. After all, they want to be there because they've shown an aptitude for English. Well, apart from the ones who've been told they have to go because they're lagging behind.'

I gulped. For a moment I considered saying 'There seems to be some kind of misunderstanding here. I think the person you're looking for is a teacher. I'm a failed IT professional. In fact, I'm a failed IT professional who doesn't like children very much.'

And then I thought that 'No job too small' had been a good motto, but 'No job too terrifying' was an even better one.

'Sounds great', I smiled.

Unchained Melody

I like the Righteous Brothers as much as any good-hearted person, but I've never been a fan of *Unchained Melody*. I like it even less now. The blame for this lies with the genius who compiled the 'New English File Elementary' coursebook for students and decided that the concepts of possessive pronouns and adjectives were ones best illustrated via the medium of the 60s soft-rock classic.

Now this might be fine with a group of students but, in one-to-one lessons, it could surely only end in mild embarrassment or, at worst, terrible misunderstanding ('No Davide, I need *your* love...I hunger for *your* touch...are you still *mine*?'). It would have been even worse with individual female students. I might as well have turned up wearing a chest wig and a medallion.

No, I was not going to do this. I would have to find another way of harnessing the power of rock to demonstrate the possessive form. One of my students told me she'd like to have a lesson based around English music. I thought I might use Hawkwind to show the difference between subject and object pronouns ('*I* am the Master of the Universe...the wind of time is blowing through *me*').

My first Business English contracts were coming to an end and I was starting to think my timetable was going to look a little thin in December and January. Then, over the course of a week, work flooded in. Hardly a day went by without the offer of another class. The logistics were becoming a nightmare. A typical day might start with a class on the Lido, following which I'd catch the boat to Piazzale Roma and then the bus out to Spinea for the afternoon, stopping off in Mestre for an evening class. If ACTV operated a 'boat miles' scheme, I'd have been coining it in.

By now we were almost at the limit of the hours that we could realistically work. We were aware that it might not always be like this and that the summer months were likely to be thin, but, for the moment, it was a nice problem to have. Our dining room table had become a repository for *Headway, Cutting Edge, New English File, In Company, Business Focus, Practical English Usage, The Practice of English Language Teaching* and the blessed Jim Scrivener's *Teaching English Grammar.* Books full of phrasal verbs and ten minute filler exercises for those awkward moments when you look at the clock and realise you're going to under-run.

It was turning out to be a very strange job. In the same week I prepared a lesson for teenagers explaining the magic of the traditional English Christmas via the music of Slade; two hours of business material for an honorary consul; and a lesson on the restoration of Jan van Eyck's *The Annunciation* (the art restorer wanted to learn some technical vocabulary). Yeah, it was certainly the strangest job I'd ever had. It was almost certainly the best, as well.

Caroline, faced every day with an army of bellowing teenagers, might not have gone as far as that. Still, she came back from teaching one Friday evening and happily announced that it had 'not been horrible.' I felt we should crack open a bottle of prosecco!

Men in Cloaks

Winter had properly arrived. The blazing heat of August and the weeks of oppressively bright blue skies were now just memories. It was bitterly cold, the kind that sinks deep into your bones. It was hard to imagine that only three months previously it had been too hot to want to sit outside.

Yet I liked the fact that it was hat, coat and scarf weather again. I liked the fact that the streets were quiet and shrouded in thick blankets of fog. I liked the fact that Piazza San Marco was no longer a no-go area. Most of all, I liked the fact that I could almost forget that I owned such a thing as a pair of shorts.

Winter suits me and those few weeks were perhaps my happiest since we arrived. There is no more enthralling city than Venice at night and I would choose a different route home whenever I returned from work, wandering the foggy, semi-lit *calli* where the only sound was that of my own footsteps.

Now, what a chap really needs to look the part on a cold winter's day, is a *tabarro*. This is a type of Venetian cloak (and also the title of the shortest and nastiest of Puccini's operas). And for the last ten years, one of the *tabarrifici* in Venice has organised a *Gran Liston* in which lovers of the *tabarro* take a stroll through the streets, cloaks a-swinging all the way.

We tagged along for part of it, beginning in the Piazza. There was the occasional break for a song and a certain amount of capering, if not all that much to see. Nevertheless, it was a good excuse for a walk and it has to be said that the *tabarro* and hat combination is a very striking one, even if the preponderance of grey-bearded men gave one the impression of having wandered into a fancy-dress party where everyone had come as Vincent Price in *Witchfinder General*.

It's a great shame that people don't wear cloaks any more, but - unless you're a vampire or a masked crimefighter - it's a difficult look to carry off. But if there's anywhere in the world where it still has its place, it has to be Venice on a foggy winter's day.

I would very much like a *tabarro* of my own. The trouble is that they all seem to be hand made and, ominously, price on application. For now, along with a hat by *Borsalino*, it will have to go on the wish list.

Christmas

Christmas in the UK begins around October time and three months of 'Be of Good Cheer. By Order' is wearisome. It's more low key in Venice. Nothing starts until December and lights and decorations only go up with a couple of weeks to go. It feels less commercial and less like hard work.

The windows of *cioccolaterie* filled up with ornate displays. Legendary wine shop, bar and *cicchetteria* 'Al Bottegon' (a place we've been coming to since 2005, and where we have built up a relationship with the staff to the level where we sometimes get a half-smile) had its usual tree constructed of wine corks. And *Presepi* started to appear in churches. The Venetians are very keen on these: nativity scenes, from the Latin *praesepium*. They go to extraordinary lengths and levels of detail in their construction. The one at San Trovaso contained two water features, fire effects and a clever bit of lighting that cycled from dawn to dusk to the dark of night. The Scalzi was in full-blown 'art installation' mode where the visitor encountered life-size Magi in an alcove on the right, from where the gaze was drawn up to a great, golden comet-like strip that lead across the vault of the roof to the Holy Family in the chapel opposite. Not to be outdone, the Frari attempted a complete immersive experience with an outdoor 'living *presepio*' with all the characters played by local children. At least that was the idea. Whenever we passed by, the *bambini* were conspicuous by their absence. I suppose if the contest was between sitting outside for hours in the cold and damp pretending to be a shepherd, or staying at home with the Xbox, there was only ever likely to be one winner. *O tempora o mores.*

Santa Maria Maddalena hosted its 22nd *Mostra del Presepio,* which provided an opportunity to have a look around a rarely open church. The sheer number and scale of them all made it difficult to get a proper impression of the interior, but there was at least the chance to see a *Last Supper* by Giandomenico Tiepolo. Many of the *presepi* themselves show biblical scenes transferred to a Venetian setting : a Doge pays homage to the Holy Family in a stable positioned in front of the Rialto bridge, as gondolas pass by in the background.

Now some of these might appear naive or merely *kitsch* at first glance, but what they're doing is conceptually no different from religious art through the ages, where biblical scenes were set against contemporary and local backgrounds, and the great and the good of the day had themselves painted in as participants in the drama (either for egotistical reasons, or in the hope that it might score bonus points when it came to the immortal soul being weighed). They're some of the most delightful Christmas sights to be seen in the city.

The choir's Christmas concert was held just two days before Christmas. It hadn't been that long since the Marcello/Bernstein performance and so was more modest in scale. It was nevertheless an interesting programme - two *Magnificats* from Arvo Part and Herbert Howells, and Gustav Holst's *Christmas Day.* Nothing in Italian, you'll notice, which put me in the strange position of general source of advice on pronunciation and translator of archaic English words.

The venue was the island of *San Lazzaro degli Armeni.* There's been a church here since the 12th century, when the island served as a quarantine station and leper colony. After falling into disuse it was gifted to the Mechitarist order of the Armenian Catholic church in 1717. It was the only monastery to be spared when Napoleon abolished the other institutions in 1810. After almost three hundred years, this tiny spit of land remains one of the great centres of Armenian scholarship.

Lord Byron spent much of 1816 here, rowing out to the island every day to talk with the brothers and learn all he could about their culture and history. Not only did he learn the language, but he also compiled a grammar, contributed to a dictionary and translated various episodes from the Bible. Now, given that he managed to do all this while still finding time to write poetry and, presumably, enjoy adventures of a suitably 'Byronic' nature, why was it taking us so bloody long just to learn Italian?

It was a cold and foggy day so - though Byron would have been appalled - the *vaporetto* was the easiest way to get out to the island. It wasn't much warmer in the church itself. But it's a beautiful, jewel-like interior and an absolutely lovely space to perform in.

Good wishes were exchanged, sparkling wine was drunk and truly ridiculous amounts of panettone were consumed in the refectory afterwards; and then it was time to head back to Venice. Feeling, once again, just that little bit more at home.

Christmas Eve was a mixture of British radio (*9 Lessons and Carols* and *The Archers*. I felt old just typing that) and Italian cooking. Our fishmonger told Caroline that the traditional Venetian meal for Christmas Eve is risotto of *volpina*, followed by roast eel; and so that's what we had. *Volpina* is one of the many words the Venetians seem to have for grey mullet and it makes for a very nice risotto indeed – a little plain, perhaps, but if you're following it up with an eel, then that's all to the good. I've never enjoyed eel all that much before (and the icky method of despatch that Mr Eel undergoes at the hands of the fishmonger did little to encourage me), but roasting it in a hot oven for 30 minutes was the way to go - the flesh was meltingly soft, the skin deliciously crisp.

Christmas dinner, by contrast, was thoroughly British: a roast goose in marmalade, with sprouts, bread sauce and red cabbage. It took hours of honest toil and sweat by myself, in a kitchen the size of a shoebox, but it was worth every minute. It went very well with a nice bottle of red wine that one of my students had bought me.

It seemed unbelievable that an entire year had passed since Christmas in South Wales. So much had changed for us in just twelve months.

Capodanno

My attempt to make toast on the morning of December 31st was scuppered by a cloud of greasy, grey smoke that came pouring out of the oven within seconds of switching the grill on. This shouldn't have surprised me given that it hadn't been cleaned since roasting an eel and a goose on consecutive days.

I had a spray around with the Italian equivalent of Mr Muscle and left it for half an hour. I returned to find the bottom of the oven covered in a thick layer of melted fat. I could feel my arteries hardening just looking at it. Cleaning it out was a less than lovely job; but I gave myself a break by scrubbing out the filter in the dishwasher as well.

We spent the afternoon on prep for next term. I put together a lesson for my students based around Hogmanay in Scotland. In other words, I described what a great time people were having in the place we left a year ago, whereas, in our new life, we were spending the day working. It seemed terribly post-modern.

New Year's Eve never used to be like this. But then, it didn't need to be the same. It used to be a final, desperate booze-up at the fag-end of the festive season; as we tried to blot out the horrible reality of going back to work. Now, it didn't seem so important. In a week's time, I'd be back at work but I loved my job and I'd be in Venice. And if Caroline loved the job somewhat less than I did; well, at least she'd be in Venice.

There was a party organised in Piazza San Marco, but it didn't sound like our sort of thing. Neither of us felt like standing around for hours in sub-zero temperatures listening to DJs. So we settled in for the evening and I cooked us the traditional Italian New Year's Eve meal of *cotechino e lenticchie*. *Cotechino* is a sausage consisting of, shall we say, miscellaneous bits of pork, salt, spices and quite a lot of fat. We'd tried its near relation *zampone* (a stuffed pig's trotter) in the past but found it just a bit too agricultural. There was some Brahms and Mahler on RAI 3 and a pause for the President's Address (the Italian equivalent of the Queen's Speech) halfway through; so I was happy just to potter away in the kitchen as Caroline caught up on her email mountain.

Dinner itself wasn't much more than OK. You might initially describe it as 'unctuous', but you'd also move swiftly on to 'a little more unctuous than you'd like'. It was quite fatty and there was no getting away from the fact that we weren't really dealing with prime cuts of meat. Still, we're prepared to give it a go next year, although I think we'll take a step up from *Billa*'s own boil-in-the-bag range. The meal is alleged to be a bringer of good luck and the *lenticchie* (lentils) are supposed to bring money. Perhaps we could just stick with the lentils?

We went up to the *altana* to watch the fireworks at midnight; enjoyable if not on the scale of *Redentore*. It had been a low-key New Year's Eve, but it didn't need to be anything more. 2012 had been the maddest, craziest year of our lives. We were allowed to finish it with a quiet night in.

I've always wanted to live within walking distance of an opera house and now we were living just five minutes' walk from *La Fenice*. It seemed so wonderfully civilised. Even more so on New Year's Day, when I could stumble out of bed at 10:00, shower, shave, make coffee, have breakfast, fret about what to wear and still be at the theatre for curtain up at 11:15.

The very first public opera house in the world was in Venice. At one time it had ten of them. *La Fenice* was built in 1792 on the site of the Teatro San Benedetto which had burned to the ground, a fate which then befell *Fenice* itself in 1836.

It is, without a doubt, one of the world's great lyric theatres. It was the site of premieres by Bellini, Rossini and Donizetti. In the 20th century, Britten, Stravinsky, Berio and Nono all wrote works for it. But the composer most associated with *La Fenice* is Giuseppe Verdi, whose *Attila, Rigoletto, La Traviata* and *Simon Boccanegra* all premiered here.

So when it burned down again in 1996 (when a pair of electricians, involved in a contractual dispute, deliberately set fire to it) there was never any doubt that it would be rebuilt. In 1836, it took just twelve months. This time around, eight years were needed. There's probably a lesson about progress in there somewhere...

The entire philosophy behind the reconstruction was *com'era, dov'era* ('as it was, where it was'). And so it is. It's quite an achievement, but whether it was the correct decision is another matter. Opinion on the new *Fenice* is mixed. Yes, it's all very pretty, but there's no getting away from the fact that this is a brilliantly realised fake and that an opportunity was missed to move away from the image of the 'museum city'. In addition, if you were to design an opera house today, you wouldn't start with the traditional horseshoe-shaped system of boxes that leaves half the audience sitting at 90 degrees to the action on stage. *La Repubblica* lamented '...the city should have had the nerve to build a completely new theatre; Venice has betrayed its innovative past by ignoring it.'

Enough carping. It is still a lovely place to go to the opera. The tradition of a New Year's Day concert only dates back to the reconstruction, but the rationale behind it is a good one: given the viewing figures for the New Year event in Vienna, why shouldn't Venice have its own? And with the spiky historical relationship between Venice and Austria, why wouldn't a programme of Verdi go down better than a programme of miscellaneous Strausses?

This year, the city had pulled off a bit of a coup. The Vienna concert was under the reliable if stolid direction of Franz Welser-

Most, but *Fenice* had a genuine star in *uber*-serious Baroque specialist John Eliot Gardiner. A surprising choice, as one tends to associate JEG with reverential treatments of Monteverdi and Bach. He didn't seem the type for the more frivolous demands of a New Year's Day concert. Everyone would have been up late. Strong drink might have been taken. We *could*, I suppose, listen to two hours of Bach and examine our relationship with God and the hereafter; but what we *really* want at 11am on January 1st are the best bits of Verdi and some stomping choruses to set us up for the year ahead. And, after a just-serious-enough first half (the *Aida* Sinfonia and Tchaikovsky's second symphony), that's what we got - a selection of Verdi's Greatest Hits.

There was an explosion of glitter at the end and a clap-along to the final *Brindisi*. JEG isn't usually one to tolerate this sort of frivolity, but he got into the spirit of the occasion and asked the soprano to join him for a quick waltz on the podium. Everyone left in good spirits, out into a cold and foggy Venetian afternoon.

A word on 'restricted view' tickets at *La Fenice*. These seem to give you a 75% chance of a view of most the stage without too much craning about and a 25% chance of being behind a pillar. On this occasion, Caroline got the pillar. I did offer to change seats, but she insisted. Still, my work in the kitchen over Christmas had built me up a stash of Hubby Points. I figured it was time to cash them in.

Something rotten in the state of Cawdor

At the front of a stage strewn with dead babies, a bloodied Macbeth flopped wearily onto the sofa, next to the corpse of his wife and expired with no more drama than as if he'd fallen asleep in front of the television. The ghost of Banquo removed the crown from the dead king's head and placed it upon that of Malcolm, who promptly vomited, violently and copiously.

Curtain.

We've seen a number of *Macbeth*s over the years. We've seen productions using the backdrop of a Dutch mental hospital; of an east European civil war; of a central African war zone. We've seen it performed in the style of *The Simpsons*; and by a cast of tiny plastic ninja figurines. Sometimes we've even seen it set in mediaeval Scotland. But we'd never seen one quite like this.

We hadn't been to the theatre for some time, despite an interesting-looking programme at the Teatro Goldoni. Then Caroline was asked to give a lesson on *Macbeth*, as one of her classes of shouty teenagers was being taken along. We hoped this meant some free tickets would be forthcoming, but it was not to be. Still, this sort of thing was right up her street: she prepared a lesson on all the wacky productions we'd seen, by way of contrast with what, we naively assumed, was going to be a more traditional setting.

The production began not on the traditional blasted heath but in the middle of a right old party *chez* Macbeth. The kingdom had been saved, the Norwegians had been put to flight and everybody was absolutely roaring drunk. In a tweak to the plot, Lady Macbeth was the first to encounter the witches, in the form of three baby dolls on the sofa. They delivered the prophecy. She laughed herself hoarse. She called Macbeth in to listen. He laughed himself hoarse. They gave Banquo a shout, he wandered in and...oh look, you've got the idea by now.

The trouble with all this is that the viewer increasingly felt like the designated driver at a party at which everyone else is having a riotous old drunken time, while he nurses his half pint and prays that nobody will attempt to talk to him.

After ten minutes, the endless braying, cackling laughter became irritating.

After twenty minutes, we started looking at our watches.

After thirty minutes we started praying that Macduff would get a move on and slaughter the whole bloody lot of them.

It wasn't all bad. When the roaring and cackling stopped (which, over the course of two hours, was not as often as you'd like) there was some good acting going on; and some of the production ideas had a certain power - the line of kings was accompanied by Lady Macbeth bloodily miscarrying three babies, a striking if queasy image.

Mercifully, it zipped along at quite a pace and before we knew it we were at 'Tomorrow and tomorrow and tomorrow...' which translates absolutely literally as 'Domani e domani e domani'. Then Macduff turned up, more dead babies were pressed into service and then, with not so much as a scuffle, it was all over and Macbeth was dead on the sofa.

It was an unsatisfying evening all round. It hadn't even been a good test of our Italian as much of the dialogue was inaudible. Caroline's students were positively traumatised by it. There were a couple of good things, but the overriding impression was very much of *una storia raccontata da un idiota, piena di rumori e di rabbia, che vuol dire...niente.*

Who is that bloodied man?

I'd had a few lesson cancellations, so I volunteered to do the weekly shop at the Santa Marta farmers' market instead of Caroline; and went along to the butcher's stall to collect the liver she'd ordered.

The *signora* recognised me as the husband of the Scottish woman (national identities had become blurred by now) and went off to look for it. She came back with a hefty looking bag.

'How much did you want?'
'Hmm, 300 grammes, maybe 400?'

She heaved the bag on to the scales. It was well over a kilo-and-a-half.

'Too much?'

'Erm, well it is really. Just a little.'

She shrugged, 'OK, no problem. Pay for 400g, we'll give you the rest.'

I walked away with a salami and one-and-a-half kilos of liver, for eight euros in total.

I set myself to work as soon as I got home. There aren't all that many ways of cooking liver other than flash-frying it, and most recipes seem to be variations on:

Liver with onions
Liver with wine
Liver Surprise (liver without onions or wine)

I also failed to find any that recommended 750g per person, so this all needed to be packed away into the freezer. I took a look inside the bag. It actually seemed to be an entire pig's liver. The butcher had said it was extremely fresh and he wasn't kidding. It was also extremely bloody. After five minutes work my hands, my knife, the chopping board and the surfaces were all soaked in blood. The kitchen looked like party night, *chez* Hannibal Lecter.

I wondered how I would explain it if somebody came to the door and drew unfortunate conclusions from my appearance, the absence of Caroline and a suspiciously well-stocked freezer.

Liver freezes very well and *Fegato alla Venezia* - with white wine vinegar and onions - is a local speciality. I could see it becoming a staple over the coming months.

It is not just a cheese – it is a weapon of the Revolution

'This chain of solidarity is wonderful: the only way to help us now is to buy parmesan cheese' - Giuseppe Alai, president of the Parmigiano-Reggiano Cheese Consortium

Approximately 300,000 wheels of Parmesan cheese were damaged during the earthquake in Emilia Romagna. They were stacked up in warehouses, where they'd been left to mature. When the earthquake hit, the stacks collapsed and many of the wheels broke open or cracked.

Now, set against the loss of life and the destruction of property and historic buildings, this might seem frivolous, but it really wasn't. Because Parmesan takes years to mature and if you found yourself with a warehouse full of cracked and damaged cheeses - you'd just seen your income for the next few years wiped out.

Then the producers came up with a possible solution. If a cheese had been damaged, the theory went, it couldn't be left to mature further, but there was no reason why it couldn't be sold now. So regional associations throughout Italy helped to set up a market for 'Earthquake Parmesan' where consumers could buy perfectly good cheese at a reduced (but not exploitative) price.

We hadn't seen any outlets for it anywhere in the city, until Caroline saw a sign outside the local office of the Communist Party. She said she was just on her way to the shops, but I like to think that she drops by every week for a quick chat about Gramsci's theory of Cultural Hegemony over tea and biscuits. She popped in and found herself in a smoke-filled room where the comrades seemed confused by her presence, until she explained that she was there to help in The Struggle and came away with a kilo of cheese.

It was absolutely first-class, with that wonderful crunchiness that the best Parmesan has. It lasted us for months, but we should have gone back and stocked up with more.

There was now only a month until the Italian election and, on the evidence so far, the Communists clearly had the best festivals and the best cheese. If we were entitled to a vote, they'd have had ours.

Carnevale

In *Life, the Universe and Everything*, Douglas Adams came up with the idea of an orbiting cocktail party that had been running for so long the partygoers were now the great-great-great-great-grandchildren of the original guests. *Carnevale*, which once stretched to six months of the year, must have felt like that.

It fell into decline from the 19th century onwards and was ultimately banned by Mussolini, never much of a party animal. It was re-introduced in 1979, but nowadays it's a more manageable week-and-a-bit.

We had yet to meet an adult Venetian who could get particularly enthused by *Carnevale,* although this was, admittedly, based on a sampling of four people. *Carnevale*, they said, was once a local event for local people, who would meet up, in costume, for music, dancing, eating and drinking. Nowadays it was no longer for Venetians, the city was too crowded and who would want to spend all that time making a costume just to be mistaken for a tourist?

Costumed people were everywhere. This was sometimes quite effective (a pair of cloaked and masked figures seen in an otherwise deserted *calle* made for a pleasingly spooky image*)* and sometimes less so (a woman in normal clothes, save for a sparkly mask, at a bus stop outside a supermarket in Mestre). On the *vaporetto* one evening I found myself standing next to a man dressed as Napoleon; something that, in Venetian terms, is akin to going to a Scotland - England game whilst dressed as the Duke of Cumberland.

It was interesting, yes, but not all that enjoyable. Piazza San Marco, near-deserted only a few days previously, once again became a seething, near-impassable mass of humanity. The *vaporetto* services were hard work. Just walking the streets was less of a pleasure than it had been. If there is a parallel to be drawn, it's with Edinburgh's Hogmanay, which, in the space of a few years, turned into a mass tourist spectacle that made the centre of town a no-go area for locals. It must be quite exciting if you have an interest in costume. If you like tricorn hats there is clearly no better place to be in February. But it's not really our thing.

Carnevalaltro, by contrast, is the stroppy younger brother of the main event. It was being held in Campo Sant'Angelo, just a few steps from our flat.

As I passed through the *campo* on my way back from work, I noticed stalls were selling beer, wine, kebabs even and some things which might have been hats. A *'No Grandi Navi'* banner was draped in front of the main stage. The festival slogan was *'Facciamo la festa all'austerity'* and the logo the stylised Guy Fawkes mask from Alan Moore's *V for Vendetta* that had become the symbol of the Occupy movement. There was an alternative, political edge to things; a nice contrast to the smug, manufactured feel of the official event.

A band was tuning up on stage. Loudly. Excessively loudly, but then, this is Venice and I thought it would all be finished by 9:00.

Wrong. It didn't get going until 10:30. The band was an electric folk/rock group (a bit like The Levellers, if anyone remembers them) accompanied by the drummer from hell. With a steady 4/4 beat in every song, he didn't have much to do, but, by God, he was going to do it LOUDLY.

It was noisy. Very, very, very noisy. Sleep was out of the question, so I wandered back to the *campo* to see what was happening. The band were playing away, the drummer hammering the crap out of his skins as if he was afraid they'd leap up and attack him if he stopped hitting them for more than a second. Behind the main stage was a projection of a recent *No Grandi Navi* demonstration, in which a small flotilla blocked the path of a giant cruise ship until they were removed by police boats and helicopter. But the square was full of young people and there was a good-natured vibe to it all.

Yeah, it was too loud, but its heart was in the right place and we probably weren't the target audience anyway. On the other hand I had to go to work the next day.

The band packed up long after midnight and the crowd, slowly and noisily, made their way home.

I was somewhat bleary-eyed in the morning but cheered myself up with the thought that it only happened once a year. And then, reading through *La Nuova*, I realised that had just been the first night. There were another five to go. Friday was Reggae Night and, again, they insisted on sharing their righteous sounds with us until the small hours. Saturday was Rock Night. Sunday seemed to be put aside for a special Festival of Drumming. And then, on Monday, we practically sobbed with relief as a combination of thick snow and *acqua alta* put paid to the festivities.

La Nuova reported that the event was a big success, even amongst the locals in the square; although the only person I know in Campo Sant'Angelo is a retired lady whose presumed love for four-hour drum solos has yet to be shared with me.

We'd been hoping the final event might be an Acoustic Guitar Night, or even a Mime Night, but, as the drums started to beat out their familiar, insistent rhythm, we realised our hopes were to be dashed. Then, after five days of hell, a team of workers arrived to start taking down the stage and the disturbingly large loudspeakers. I felt a strange urge to give them a hug, or at least to lend them a hand. Just to be absolutely sure.

The harsh weather never seemed to deter the hardier Carnival-goers. Caroline saw another Napoleon on the *vaporetto*, stoically sitting outside on his own, gazing into the horizontal snow as if contemplating the retreat from Moscow.

Schools get time off for *Carnevale* and half my private students were either off ill or on holiday. There wasn't much work to detain us but a combination of the weather and the crowds kept us largely indoors, sulking and eating *fritelle*.

Ah yes, *fritelle*. Or, 'what they don't tell you about the Italian diet'. We'd been grumpy about the whole festival experience, but there was at least one good thing that came out of it, and that was the discovery of these little doughnuts. They come in various forms, from the traditional unfilled *Fritelle Veneziane*, to varieties filled with pastry cream or *zabaglione*. When they're good, they're very, very good indeed. And when they're bad, hell, they're still pretty good. They're only supposed to be available during *Carnevale* and rightly so. Short of giving away free cigarettes, it's harder to think of a greater risk to public health.

We became obsessed with them. No venture outside was complete without a visit to a new shop to work our way through their selection. Every choir practice ended with huge trays of them being unwrapped and the popping of prosecco corks. I considered creating a league table on a dedicated spreadsheet.

Then *Carnevale* came to an end and, sadly, so did our supply of doughnuts. We felt strangely bereft for the first few days, but that was probably just our bodies adjusting to the sudden lack of sugar. They're clearly from Satan's very own deep-fat fryer but they improved the carnival experience for us no end. Some Venetians leave the city during the festive period, but that seems a little excessive. Next year we might just stock up on *fritelle*, soundproof the flat as best we can and stay indoors for the whole eleven days.

Election Fever

'We are the first party, but we have lost '- Pierluigi Bersani.

'The people have spoken, the bastards' - Dick Tuck, 1966 Senate

election, California.

Mario Monti's interim government had finally fallen and an election was due. We were not, of course, entitled to a vote; which was possibly just as well. If British politics has become a straightforward choice between two cheeks of the same bottom; then the Italian system - with its raft of parties and coalitions, and a dreadful electoral system commonly referred to as *Porcellum* ('the pig sty') - is Byzantine in its complexity. It took some time to make sense of it all, as this was more than a simple contest between left and right. There were four main players in the game :

Pierluigi Bersani's *Partito Democratico* (PD) - the main party of the *centrosinistra*, in an alliance with Nichi Vendola's *Sinistra Ecologia Liberta* (SEL) and a number of smaller parties of the left. Bersani seemed a decent enough bloke if not terribly exciting, but a not-terribly-exciting leader was perhaps what Italy needed. Vendola, proudly gay, Catholic and Marxist, was a more charismatic figure; albeit significantly more popular than his actual party.

Silvio Berlusconi's *Popolo della Liberta* (PDL) - the *centrodestra*, in a coalition with Roberto Maroni's *Lega Nord* and a number of small right-wing parties of varying degrees of unpleasantness.

Mario Monti's *Scelta Civica* - a coalition led by Monti, with support from various centrist parties, technocrats and clever people. His technocratic government was always far more popular with the markets than with Italians, but there was at least a feeling that he was a fundamentally decent man; and someone who could safely be sent off to meet with foreign heads of state without acting like Peter Sellers in an old Blake Edwards film.

Beppe Grillo's *Movimento Cinque Stelle* (M5S) - an 'anti-political' movement started by Grillo, a former TV comedian. Grillo had charisma to burn and filled piazzas wherever he went, but there remained doubt as to whether M5S was just a slightly weird personality cult; or if offered anything more than a protest vote for the huge number of voters sick of the current system.

A couple of the smaller parties also deserve a mention. *CasaPound* is named after American poet and celebrity fascist Ezra Pound. Their symbol, oddly, is a turtle: swastikas, it seems, are *passé*. The name translates as 'Ezra Pound's House'. I wondered how scary they could be. After all, the vicar of the Anglican church in Venice lives next door to Ezra Pound's house and he's a splendid chap. The answer is 'very scary indeed' - one of their election posters consisted of nothing but the message 'You have been too tolerant for too long.' Thankfully, they had a minuscule amount of support.

Revoluzione Civile was a coalition of the left headed by the anti-mafia prosecutor Antonio Ingroia, in connection with some reformist/anti-corruption parties, as well as the Communists and the Greens. They seemed an interesting bunch. However, in the grand tradition of left-wing politics, they didn't get on with the other left-wing parties and wouldn't talk to them.

Then, of course, there was Silvio. *Il Cavaliere* was over every TV channel like a rash. It's possible Pope Benedict's resignation was just a desperate attempt to get him off the news for a few days. In the meantime, he'd been his usual self. He slept through the service on Holocaust Memorial Day, waking up just in time to suggest that Mussolini was not such a bad chap after all. He sleazed his way revoltingly through an interview with a female employee of an energy company. He sent out missives in official-looking envelopes in marginal areas saying the bearers would be able to take them to a bank in order to receive a complete reimbursement of Monti's hated property tax.

But there was still a hard-core who would vote for him. Silvio, they would say, protects us from the communists. Politicians are thieves, but Silvio is a businessman. But what about the criminal convictions? Ah, the judges are all communists. What about the sleazy sexual allegations? All made by feminists or communists!

Bersani? Communist! Monti? He only cares about the Germans! But Silvio...Silvio cares about Italy.

The Germans wanted Monti. The French wanted Bersani. The markets would have been happy with either, or both, or anyone as long as it wasn't Silvio. What everybody wanted was stability. And stability is the opposite of what they got...

On a late bus from Mestre on election night a drunk was busy telling the rest of the passengers how pleased he was that Beppe Grillo and M5S had got 25% of the vote. It seemed hard to believe. Did he mean nationally or in the Veneto? Was my Italian just a bit wonky? Or was he, as seemed most likely, just a drunk bloke determined to entertain us all on the way back to Venice? I stuck my face in my book and tried desperately to avoid any eye contact with him.

He was, of course, completely right.

Berlusconi's vote, and that of the Lega, was almost half that of 2008. The trouble was that the PD vote also declined dramatically. In the end, *Il Cavaliere* did what he had to do: he shored up his core vote enough and, together with his coalition partners, was able to deny the left a majority.

Bersani never made his presence felt. Berlusconi and Grillo are masters at the communication game and there was a large degree of interest from the press in Monti's campaign. The feeling was that Bersani never attempted to seize the agenda and was happy to sit back and wait for victory to drop into his lap.

Monti himself cut a diminished figure as a politician instead of a technocrat. Had he really wanted to run at all? Tellingly, his vote from overseas voters was twice what he received at home.

Grillo spent much of the post-election period as he spent the pre-election period: bellowing himself purple and insulting people. Yet, if you stripped away the oafishness and the coarseness, he did have a few reasonable ideas and his suggestion of Dario Fo as President of the Republic was an inspired one (Fo - 87 years old – unfortunately, but understandably, declined).

There seemed no way out of the impasse, short of another interim technocratic government; and new elections sooner rather than later. And so Bersani chose the most realistic option remaining to him: he proposed a broad alliance with Grillo. There was a reasonable degree of common ground, at least when it came to political reform. Grillo's considered response to this was *'You have a face like an arse!'*

The numbers in Parliament made it impossible to elect a President of the Republic and Bersani resigned after the humiliating defeat of his proposal, former premier and EU president Romano Prodi. Finally, outgoing president Giorgio Napolitano agreed to stay on. The 87-year old Napolitano, a decent and honourable man, had desperately wanted to retire, but agreed to return on condition that the PD and PDL would provide some kind of stability by working together in a grand coalition. If they failed, he warned, he would drag them to account for their failures before all of Italy.

After choir practice one evening, a bottle of prosecco was opened and we shared a bitter toast to *ingovernabilità*. Somewhere on high, Garibaldi must have put his head in his hands and wondered if it had been worth all the trouble.

Picasso's Revenge

For all that I loved the job, I found Mondays hard work. I would leave the house at 8:30, returning after 11:00 at night. I wasn't going to complain about too much work but, unfortunately, the weather gods had decreed that Mondays would henceforth be known as Rain Days. Because it rained all the bloody time. There are few things more depressing than emerging into the rain from a nice warm classroom, putting a cold and soggy hat on your head and realising that you are still 8 hours from a pair of dry socks. There was some blessed relief when it decided to start snowing instead, which somehow seemed marginally less wet.

Still, the job itself continued to be good fun. I found myself teaching a lot of CLIL classes after Christmas. CLIL, or Content and Language Integrated Learning, is a variation on conventional English teaching in that you teach a subject as well as the language. In the space of a few weeks I taught lessons on apartheid, nuclear physics, the economic crisis and the Italian women's movement - all in English - to Italian schoolkids. It was hard work as it took a lot of prep, but it was enormously interesting and enjoyable. Then, wonderfully, I landed my dream job - teaching classes in Art History.

The *professoressa* suggested that I start with a lesson on Picasso's *Guernica* and use some extracts from Simon Schama's TV series *The Power of Art*. This, I thought, was too ambitious, but I managed to find a version with English subtitles which would help them a little.

I started off by talking about the Spanish civil war, the Republicans, the Nationalists and Franco. I asked them if they knew who supported the Nationalists.

'Germany', somebody volunteered.

'Very good', I said, before pausing and adding, *sotto voce*, '...and Italy.'

I showed them some video clips. A lot of it was over their heads, but the scenes of the aftermath at Guernica interspersed with images of the painting gave them a general idea.

I started describing each element - if the horse represents the Spanish people, then the bull represents Franco. That sort of thing. Then I moved to the figure in the foreground.

'So what's this?'

'It's a man, prof.'

'That's right. Perhaps he's one of the innocent people at Guernica. Now what's this?' I started to think a laser pointer would be really cool at this point, but I did my best with a pen.

'*Una spada*, prof?'

'That's right, in English we call it a *sword*. What else?'

It's broken.'

'Good. It's broken. What does that mean?'

'Defeat?'

'Yes, the broken sword is a symbol of defeat. Now what's this?'

'A flower.'

'A flower – signifying...?'

'Hope?'

'Exactly! The figure is next to the *sword* which signifies *defeat* and the *flower* which signifies *hope.'*

This was going better than I thought. I moved on.

'Now let's look at his arm and his hand. What's this mark in the centre of his hand?'

Silence.

I tried again, 'It's a wound - *una ferita* - in the centre of his hand. What do you think that means?'

Silence.

'OK. Think of religious art. What do we call a wound in the centre of the hand?'

Silence.

Time for Plan B.

'OK then. Where did Picasso come from?'

'Spain?'

Spain. And where was Guernica?'

'In Spain?'

'In Spain. Now, what religion are the people of Spain?'

Silence.

'Do they have the same religion as Italy?'

Silence.

This was like pulling teeth. The *Professoressa* stared at them and shook her head in disbelief.

'What religion are the people of Italy?'

Silence, and then a wavering voice, '...Catholic?'

'Catholic, yes! The same as in Spain. So Picasso knew, if he showed an image of a hand with a wound in the centre, people would know exactly what it meant...and that is...?'

Silence.

I considered adopting a crucifixion pose, but something told me that might be a step too far. I threw them a bone instead.

'Right, we would call these marks the *stigmata*. Who does that make you think of?'

Light dawned

'Gesu Cristo?'

'Jesus Christ!!', I managed not to shout, 'It signifies the martyrdom of Jesus Christ.'

And so, blessedly, we moved on. Picasso might have thought the symbolism was obvious but he never had to deal with a class of 13 year olds.

I Don't Like Mondays

...or, why I owe the Italian train service one euro...

It was that rarest of Mondays, one that dawned without any prospect of rain. It did, however, bring with it a transport strike (only older readers will remember when British people were allowed to go on strike, but they're not that uncommon over here), meaning restricted hours of service on all *vaporetti* and buses in the area.

Which is why I found myself in Mestre at 8:30 in the morning, for a class that started at 10:15. It was an opportunity for a leisurely breakfast, but, try as you might, you can't really linger over an espresso and a croissant. Still, it was a chance to get some prep done prior to lessons starting.

Monday afternoons usually saw me heading over to Spinea for after-school classes, but they'd been cancelled. And there was no point in trying to get home, as I'd be needing to head out again as soon as I'd stuck my head round the door.

This left me with an afternoon to kill in Mestre. Poor, unloved Mestre. Truth be told, it's not all that bad and parts of the town centre are quite nice. But I didn't think it was going to keep me occupied for five hours, so I decided to plan my journey home for after my evening class. There are areas of Mestre where you might not want to linger for too long after dark and the tech where I taught was a fair way out of town. If I was going to have to walk all the way to the railway station, I wanted to have the route clear in my mind.

It took a bit of working out, but the only tricky stretch was the underpass near the station. I was probably being paranoid, but, given I'd just picked up my month's pay, I was twitchy about walking around lonely, unlit areas. After a busy March, I found myself with a veritable *bella cifra* of cash in my wallet. It would have been a really, really bad day to get mugged. Still, I consoled myself, one of my nice students would give me a lift.

Ah. So you're all going in different directions then? Nowhere near the station? Not possible to make a short detour? No? No, no worries, I'll be fine, don't worry about me. Just count yourselves lucky I'm not the one marking your exams.

So off I strode, with as much confidence as a man in a cardigan with a 'man bag' is able to project. Down Via Miranese. Under the flyover. Towards the station and the underpass. No-one else around. Deserted. Or was it? I tried to keep the words of The Jam's *Down in the Tube Station at Midnight* out of my head as I rounded a scary blind corner and then I was up the other side and could see the welcoming lights of the station in the distance. I'd made it. All I had to do now was pass through the red-light district that occupies this stretch of road without making eye-contact with anyone and I'd be nearly home.

The ticket office at the station was closed. As was the newspaper stand that sells tickets for the Mestre-Venezia route. I found a machine but it was out of order. There had to be another one, but there was a train at the platform by now and I was going to miss it unless...*oh to hell with it*, I thought, *they never check on this stretch, just get on it, you'll be fine.*

I settled into my seat for a read of the paper when a movement caught my eye. A guard was inexorably making his way through the carriage, checking tickets. This was, I suppose, inevitable. I'd been working all day, it was pushing 11:00 and now I was going to be fined god-knows-how-much for the sake of a one euro ticket.

I made my way to the next carriage down, heading away from the guard. And then the next. And the next. I felt like Robert Donat in *The Thirty Nine Steps*.

Of course, Robert Donat extricated himself from the situation by hurling himself upon an unsuspecting Madeleine Carroll. I glanced around the carriage. The only other occupant was a bored-looking street vendor with a bag full of fake Louis Vuittons. He didn't look like Madeleine Carroll. Even if he had, I thought any sort of hurling would end badly. I continued making my way along the train.

The Mestre-Venezia journey takes just ten minutes, yet time seemed to pass at a glacial pace. We arrived just before I ran out of carriages, and I blessed the Italians and their extremely long trains. I felt bad about not paying, but there wasn't an honesty box for me to deposit a euro in.

A few people were waiting at the number 2 *vaporetto* stop as there'd been a sporadic service earlier that evening. A bus home would have been a welcome treat, so I decided to hang around just in case. Fifteen minutes later someone official-looking arrived and told us there'd be no more services that night. It had, of course, started to rain in the meantime.

It was a miserable, damp walk home, but I was on the last stretch and then...and then it turned out there'd been unexpected *acqua alta* and Calle della Mandorla was flooded. If I had been thinking straight, I would have realised that there was a stretch of

191

passarelle that I could use just around the corner, but I wasn't thinking straight. I was, quite successfully, working myself into A Bit of a State. This was obviously karma. I'd defrauded the Italian train service of a euro and now I was going to have to pay. I rolled up my trouser legs and strode forth...

It was 11:30 by the time I squelched back into the flat. Caroline was long since asleep. I plopped my soggy socks into the laundry basket and poured myself a large, large glass of red wine. Next Monday, I told myself, next Monday would be better.

Part 6

One Year On

Jan Morris memorably describes the experience of living in Venice as one of the greatest pleasures that life can offer. Caroline's description of our first year was more prosaic, but heartfelt in its honesty: *'I didn't expect it to be difficult'*. There is, of course, some truth in both these viewpoints.

March 4th 2013 came and went. One year had passed since we arrived and sat outside a bar in an increasingly chilly Campo San Barnaba, trying not to become too concerned as the shadows lengthened and the agent for our flat obstinately refused to answer the phone. Let's take stock, then, of our first year in Venice.

Stating the obvious, it's not like being on holiday. No matter how well you think you know a place as a visitor, it will be different as a resident. No matter how well you think you know the language, there will come a time when you feel stymied because you can't think of the word for 'bleach' or 'dishwasher tablets' or 'printer cartridge'. Nothing sums up the initial frustrations of shopping as much as the time we dithered for ten minutes over which variety of grapefruit juice to buy. Grapefruit juice. Ten minutes. Repeat that for every item on the shopping list.

So we're not always doing lovely things or having an exciting time. It's perfectly possible that a week will pass without doing anything more interesting than working or preparing for work. On those days when we find ourselves plugging away at lesson plans whilst the rain hammers on the dark streets outside, it's easy to start thinking that we could be anywhere. 'New Life' is, in some ways, very similar to 'Old Life'.

Except it's not. Not really. When I get the boat to the Lido and look back and see the Alps on the horizon, it reminds me that nothing about this experience will ever, surely, seem quite normal. And if it does, if the day ever comes when we walk over the Accademia bridge without looking left or right...well, perhaps that'll be a sign that we truly belong here.

Work, surprisingly, was never that much of a problem. Or maybe the adage is true, that nothing generates work as much as being in it. Caroline quickly secured a proper contract and as soon as I had a couple of jobs under my belt, work rolled in steadily. We were lucky, though, in that we ended up with professional organisations that paid properly and on time. A quick internet search on TEFL and Italy will bring back page after page of horror stories of fly-by-night language schools and of teachers not being paid on time, or at all. We personally know people who are consistently paid months in arrears and have to fight for every last cheque. If that had happened to us, we might well have considered cutting our losses and going back to the UK.

I found the work itself rewarding and enjoyable, but it doesn't suit everybody. It is not an easy way to make a living. We'd both imagined that the job would involve giving private lessons to small groups of polite, motivated adult learners. That's only part of it. A larger part of the experience involves being thrown into a bear pit of bored, contemptuous and, above all, loud Italian teenagers; trying desperately to impart what little knowledge you can to the few interested ones, whilst hoping to emerge at the end of the lesson with both your dignity and hearing intact.

Is it possible to live in the most extraordinary city on earth on an EFL teacher's salary? The honest answer is – we don't know yet. Possibly. Certainly, it would be very difficult on a single income – you would need to flatshare and watch every last cent. On a double salary, things start to look more manageable. Still, you have to bear in mind that you will only have a guaranteed income for nine or ten months of the year. Can you make a living from teaching English? Yes. The trouble is that you can't make a *good* living from it; and, at some point over the next few years, we will have to address this.

One problem, of course, with a job that necessitates speaking English 90% of the time, is that it limits the opportunity to speak Italian. Which brings me to the issue of language.

If there is one piece of advice that I could give to those who might think of trying something similar, it would be this: your enjoyment of the experience will be in direct proportion to your knowledge of Italian. No ifs, no buts, you simply have to learn it. You can get by without very *much* in a city like Venice, but you'll never feel at home without it. I arrived with an attitude of Robespierresque severity: everything, from the date of arrival, would be in Italian. Newspapers, books, radio - all in Italian. Nothing in English. Except for *The Archers*. And *Doctor Who*. Oh, and *Forbrydelsen*, but given that was in Danish with English subtitles, that didn't count. With hindsight, this was over-the-top. It doesn't do any harm to read an English paper or watch some English television once in a while.

A number of well-meaning people have told us that you don't need to speak particularly good Italian and the level of English spoken is enough to make it unnecessary. This is very much not our experience. Yes, a large number of people in Venice speak English to a good level. I also have some highly-educated friends who cannot string a sentence together. We have needed to speak Italian for the practicalities of moving here, for medical purposes and just for getting by day-to-day.

Add to that the cultural reasons, or, as Goethe said, 'he who speaks two languages lives two lives.' What he meant, of course, is that speaking a language will open you up to a whole new culture and literature. If you do not speak the language, if you cannot read a newspaper, the country will remain foreign to you. This is less of a problem now than it was during my first stay in Italy, when the nightly one-hour broadcast from the World Service was my only contact with the homeland. With native-language television, radio and newspapers available via the internet, not to mention a sizeable English-speaking expat community; there is no need to feel cut off. I'm not saying that making use of these is wrong, only that, for me at least, this is not making the most of the opportunity.

Learning a language is akin to owning a crackly transistor radio, from which occasionally coherent sounds emerge; with the aspiration, one day, to own a wide-screen high-definition television. At the moment it feels like we have a not-very-good colour set, that occasionally needs a kick to get it going, but which, on the whole, serves its purpose.

The very things that make Venice such an enthralling place to visit also contribute to making it a difficult place to live. The disadvantage of being in the most beautiful city on the planet is that it sometimes feels as if everyone on the planet is in town. It would be untrue to say that tourism has brought no benefits to Venice; it would be equally untrue to say that its influence has been entirely benign. And one disadvantage for the expat is that it can take a long, long time before people will start to accept you as a local. Even now, after eighteen months, we still find ourselves having to explain that we are not tourists, we live and work here. It's not badly meant when people assume you're just passing through – it's just what the vast majority of people with a foreign accent are doing.

Then, of course, there is the question of the 'dying city'. Not 'is Venice sinking?' - that's not something that is going to affect anyone reading this book in their lifetime. No, the problem is one of migration. In Campo San Bartolomeo, a chemist's shop displays an LED screen with the population of the city. At the time of writing, it read 57, 980. Fifty years ago, it would have been double that. As property prices increase, rents start to become unaffordable for locals. If you happen to have inherited a property from your parents, the temptation is to sell up and move to the mainland where you can buy a bigger house for less money. In addition, living on the mainland allows you to have a car and, if you have a car, the range of work available to you increases. Add to this the day-to-day difficulties of living in a small city jammed with thousands of tourists – the packed streets, the overcrowded *vaporetti*, the closing of useful shops to be replaced with souvenir outlets – and you start to understand why, year on year, the population declines further.

I lived in Holland, many years ago now, and once visited a town called Marken where many of the locals still wore traditional Dutch costume. It was a strange experience. It wasn't a museum, but the atmosphere was of visiting a town under glass. Yet Venice has managed to avoid this by embracing the new. The city has reinvented itself – if not to everybody's taste – as a capital of contemporary culture: scarcely a month goes by without some kind of celebration of music, architecture, film, dance or art.

Perhaps, then, everyone is being too pessimistic. There are still schools in Venice, universities and plenty of young people. The city has, after all, been in decline for over four hundred years now and people were probably moaning then that it wasn't what it used to be.

So here we are, just over one year on. In April 2013 we signed up for another year in the same flat. It's more expensive than we can realistically afford on a long-term basis, but, as the employment situation has worked out better than I hoped, we thought we could treat ourselves to another year of gracious living. I feel as if we've run across a busy road and got away with it. Because there was never any guarantee that this was going to work. Oh, I thought there was a reasonable chance that it *might*, but I was prepared for the fact that we might not be able to find jobs at all, in which case we would just have to treat the whole experience as a year off before trying somewhere else in Italy. Or, in the worst case, come crawling back to the UK and do whatever it is that de-skilled middle-aged IT workers do in the middle of an economic crisis. Instead of which, we're here for the foreseeable future. And one year would not have been enough. It's only now that we're starting to make friends. Leaving now would feel frustrating, incomplete, a tale half-told.

Part of me regrets that we will never again have the experience of waiting for our flight from Heathrow and realising that for the first time in our adult lives we no longer possessed a key for anything; or of waking up to the sound of the bells of the *Carmini* the following morning, with the future seeming full of possibilities. Yet how fortunate we are to have had such an experience at all.

We enjoyed an Easter break in the UK, but it was good to be reminded of where we really wanted to be. It was late evening when we arrived back at Marco Polo and the air felt just that little bit warmer, as if spring was finally arriving. The *capitano* on the Alilaguna boat back into town was a cheerful fellow, listening to opera as he drove us down an almost-deserted Grand Canal. I thought what a nice job that must be at times. Two tourists were excitedly leaning out of the windows as far as they could, taking photographs and exclaiming at everything.

I envied them. They were seeing it all for the first time.

Glossary

Detailed here are those terms not directly explained in the text itself. For reasons of clarity, I have used the Italian spelling instead of the Venetian whenever a choice exists.

ACTV: *Azienda del Consorzio Trasporti Veneziano*. The company responsible for public transportation throughout Venice.

Acqua Alta: literally 'high water', usually in spring or autumn and due to a combination of high tides, the phase of the moon and prevailing winds from the south.

Altana: a wooden terrace erected above a rooftop, serving as an outside seating area.

Bacino: the wide expanse of water in front of the ducal palace, where the Grand Canal and Giudecca canal widen into the lagoon. Often referred to as the *Bacino di San Marco*.

Borsa crolla: 'stockmarket collapses'. Often seen paired with *lo spread vola*. A headline that became distressingly familiar both before and after our move to Italy.

Calle: pl. *calli*. Venetian name for a street or alley.

Campo: lit. 'field'. The name given to squares and public spaces throughout the city. *Piazza San Marco* is the notable exception.

Il Cavaliere: 'the cavalier', a common nickname for Silvio Berlusconi, used by friends and enemies alike.

Centrodestra: in political terms, the centre-right.

Centrosinistra: in political terms, the centre-left.

Centro Storico: the historic centre, or oldest part, of a city.

Chiesa: church.

Giardini: the public gardens in the east of the city; laid out during

201

the Napoleonic period and used to host the Architecture and Art Biennales.

Lardo: a type of *charcuterie*, made from the cured back fat of a pig.

Liston: *far el liston*, in Venetian, is to take a *passeggiata* – a stroll or walk, typically through the main square.

Moto ondoso: wave motion. In Venice, the term is used to describe the damaging waves caused by motorboats travelling at excessive speed.

No Grandi Navi: lit. 'no big ships'. An organisation campaigning against the passage of enormous, environmentally damaging cruise ships through the Giudecca canal and the *bacino*.

Passerelle: temporary raised walkways that allow the pedestrian to move around the city during periods of *aqua alta*.

Sacra Conversazione: lit. 'Sacred Conversation'. Typically, a depiction of the Madonna and Child in the company of a number of saints.

Seppie: cuttlefish.

Sestiere: district or borough. The six *sestieri* of Venice are Cannaregio, Castello, San Marco, San Polo, Santa Croce and Dorsoduro.

Sopressa: a typical style of salami from the Veneto.

Sportello: a window, or counter.

Straniero: pl. *stranieri*. A foreigner, or stranger.

La Settima Arte: 'the seventh art', or film; a suitably reverential term given the Italian love of cinema.

Vaporetto: a boat that serves as a waterbus in the city.

Vongole: clams.

Further Reading

There is no shortage of reading material, both fact and fiction, about *La Serenissima*. The following is a selection of those books that I have found particularly useful, and of those that have given me the greatest pleasure.

Jan Morris, *Venice.* Surely the most enthralling book ever written about the city; wonderfully literate and packed with information. How I would love to have lived in the city during the period she describes so beautifully.

Marcel Proust, *In Search of Lost Time.* Is there any better description of the experience of the first-time visitor to the city? Proust's Venice is possibly even more magical than the real thing.

Daphne du Maurier, *Don't Look Now.* Claustrophobic, melancholy little chiller from the short story collection *Not After Midnight.* Walk the streets alone at night and try to keep the image of the little figure in red out of your mind.

Giorgio Vasari, *The Lives of the Artists.* Vasari never quite understood the art of *La Serenissima*, believing it fundamentally inferior to that of his native Florence. Nevertheless, his chapters on Venetian art, and his account of a visit to Titian in the company of Michelangelo, are well worth reading.

John Ruskin, *The Stones of Venice.* Enormously erudite, comprehensive in its detail and often surprisingly witty and scathing, Ruskin's masterwork is perhaps more for dipping into than reading cover-to-cover; but it's an enormously useful reference work to have to hand.

HC Robbins Landon and John Julius Norwich, *Five Centuries of Music in Venice.* A comprehensive history of Venetian music, recounted in greater detail and far more eruditely than I could ever hope to.

Tiziano Scarpa, *Venice is a Fish*. A quirky, humorous account of Venice and the Venetians from an excellent writer.

Caroline Prosser, *Living and Working in Italy.* The most useful book I found on the practicalities and problems of making a move to Italy.

The Silver Spoon. The alpha and omega of Italian cookery. The sheer number of recipes packed into its 1500 pages can make it a rather dry read; but it's absolutely essential as a reference.

Francesco da Mosto, *Francesco's Kitchen.* This is one of surprisingly few English language cookbooks dedicated to Venetian cuisine. Engagingly written, with plenty of history in amongst the recipes.

Alan Davidson, *Mediterranean Seafood.* A peerless guide to seafood cookery. Davidson details each species of fish, importantly listing local names, together with a series of recipes. Erudite, informative and fascinating. Read it, even if you never cook a single recipe from it.

With Thanks

Caroline and Philip would like to thank their friends from Scottish Opera, the Scottish Arts Club, the Scottish Wine Society and the Edinburgh Bach Choir for all the years of conviviality. We miss you all.

We would like to thank the organisers and members of *Spin*, a contemporary art group run by the National Galleries of Scotland, without whom we might never have come to Venice in the first place.

To all those we never got the chance to say goodbye to - we're sorry. We simply ran out of time.

To those we've lost touch with over the years - again, we're sorry. We should have made more effort.

To those friends from our previous life at the bank - thank you for making things less horrible than they might otherwise have been. You know who you are.

We are enormously grateful to the Italian Cultural Institute of Edinburgh, who gave us a bursary to study at the *Istituto Venezia*; and to the Randolph School of Edinburgh, where we retrained as English teachers.

To the Man in the Pub – thank you, wherever you are.

To those who expressed their support and offered all sorts of help when they heard what we were up to - a massive thank you. Without you, we might well have given up the whole idea as insane. It might very well have *been* insane, but we still did it. And no, we were not being brave - we just did something we really wanted to do.

About the Author

Philip Gwynne Jones was born in Swansea in 1966. His love of Italy and all things Italian began in 1994, when he spent some time working for the European Space Agency in Frascati; a job that was less interesting than you might imagine.

After a long career as a not-very-good computer programmer, he now makes a living as a modestly good teacher of English. He lives and works in Venice with his wife, Caroline.

Follow The Project at http://jonesesavenezia.blogspot.it/

6258348R00123

Printed in Great Britain
by Amazon.co.uk, Ltd.,
Marston Gate.